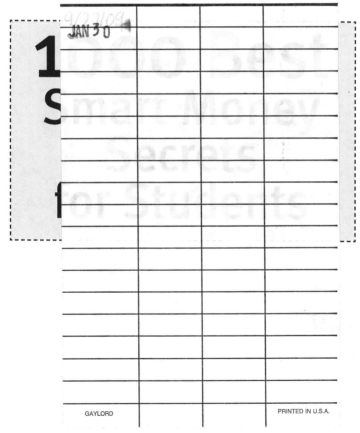

DATE DUE			FEB 06
JAN 30			
GAYLORD			PRINTED IN U.S.A.

1000 Best
Smart Money
Secrets
for Students

Debby Fowles

SOURCEBOOKS, INC.®
NAPERVILLE, ILLINOIS

Published by Sourcebooks, Inc.
P.O. Box 4410, Naperville, Illinois   60567-4410
(630) 961-3900
FAX: (630) 961-2168
www.sourcebooks.com

Library of Congress Cataloging-in-Publication Data
Fowles, Debby.
  1000 best smart money secrets for students / Debby Fowles.
    p. cm.
  ISBN 1-4022-0548-1 (alk. paper)
  1. Finance, Personal--United States. 2. College students--Finance, Per-
sonal--United States. I. Title: One thousand best smart money secrets for
students. II. Title.

HG179.F65 2005
332.024'0088'378198--dc22
                                                    2005016580

Printed and bound in the United States of America
VP 10 9 8 7 6 5 4 3 2

Dedication

To my family and loyal friends: you raise me up.

Table of Contents

Acknowledgements...................................ix

Introduction.......................................xi

Chapter 1: Good Ideas for Making Money 1

Chapter 2: Maximize Your Financial Aid 17

Chapter 3: Maximize Your Scholarships 37

Chapter 4: Understand and
            Control Credit Card Use 57

Chapter 5: How to Be Smart and Safe
            about Credit Card Debt.................. 75

Chapter 6: Manage Your Student Loans 109

Chapter 7: Save Money When Paying
            for Your Education..................... 123

Chapter 8: Mind over Money...................... 145

Chapter 9: Born to Shop? Think Again 161

Chapter 10: Miscellaneous Money-Saving Tips...... 181

Chapter 11: Live Thrifty Now.................... 215

Chapter 12: Having Fun without a Lot of Dough 257

Chapter 13: Scout out Student Discounts. 289

Chapter 14: Get the Most Bang from Your Bank 295

Chapter 15: Save Money as a Nontraditional
            or Graduate Student 311

Chapter 16: Smart Thinking at Tax Time. 327

Index 337

About the Author 353

Acknowledgments

It took a village to make this book possible:

My family, whose encouragement over the years has given me the confidence to write: my parents, Donald and Cora Fowles, sisters Becky Dow and Karen Sellner, brother Don Fowles, sister-in-law Elizabeth Fowles, and brother-in-law Randy Sellner.

My faithful friends, especially Cynthia Edmonds, the most loyal of supporters, and her daughter Aubrey, a 10-year-old financial guru; Pamela Geisbert and Carol Hoffman, whose friendship remains strong despite time and distance; Kim Knox Beckius, my About.com buddy who has taught me much; Michael Gagné, friend and employer, who provided the flexibility that makes my second career as a writer possible; my coworkers, who are like a second family; and to all the others who are always standing in my circle.

Many thanks to my wonderful agent, Barb Doyen, and my editor, Bethany Brown, who believe in me and keep the opportunities coming.

Introduction

The cost of your college education depends on many choices you make, including whether you attend a public or private school, an in-state or out-of-state school, the school's location, and whether you decide to live at home, off campus, or in the dorms. These decisions, plus many less obvious but no less critical ones, will determine how much you end up paying for your degree and how much debt you'll have to deal with after you graduate.

More and more college students are getting into serious debt that has little to do with their education and much to do with the lifestyle they choose while in college, and their use of credit cards and student loan money to pay for basic expenses, entertainment, and discretionary items. Taking advantage of every opportunity to earn or save money—from working summers or part-time while attending classes, to saving windfalls like cash gifts and income tax refunds—can make a significant dent in the amount of money you have to borrow. Every dollar you don't have to borrow is a dollar you don't have to repay and pay interest on.

How you handle money impacts every area of your life, including your personal relationships, so controlling your finances will empower you in other areas of your life as well. Just as you delayed gratification in high school in order to study hard enough to get the grades that got you into college, now is the time to fight the temptation to carelessly spend your earnings, savings, scholarships, and student loan money. Before you know it, your four years of college will be over, and you'll be living with the accumulated consequences of every financial decision you made in college.

The problems that loom largest over your financial future are credit card debt and student loan debt. While student loans can be "good" debt because they're an investment in your future, if you don't control your spending carefully, that "good" debt turns into ugly debt that will feel like a heavy anchor you have to hold onto for many years.

Studies show that the average high school graduate lacks fundamental money management skills and a basic understanding of how credit and money work. It's up to you to take your future in your own hands and teach yourself the skills necessary to prevent you from stumbling through your financial life through trial and error. The more you educate yourself about the cost of your choices, large and small, the more control you'll have over the cost of your education, and the more you'll be able to enjoy your new career after graduation. Consider your education in personal finance every bit as critical to your future success as the core classes required for your major.

Take responsibility for your financial future by using as many of the thousand money-saving tips in this book as possible, and you'll be able to truly enjoy the excitement and sense of accomplishment you've earned when you graduate with manageable debt and no regrets.

1.

Good Ideas for Making Money

Working part-time while you're in school can mean the difference between living like a pauper or enjoying some of the creature comforts your parents provided for you while you were living at home. Whether you work summers only, part-time on or off campus during the school year, or you decide to be your own boss, these moneymaking tips will help you get started.

1. Start saving some of your earnings early, preferably while you're still in high school. Once you're in college and struggling to make ends meet, you'll wish you had some of that money you spent on eating out, cell phone bills, gas, CDs, and clothes. Put away a percentage of your earnings and gift money in a special savings account earmarked for college.

2. If you don't want to detract from your study time by working while you're in college, beef up your summer job savings by working at a job that allows overtime. Because your employer is required to pay you time-and-a-half for any hours you work over forty in a week, your overtime dollars will add up fast. Work as much overtime as you can, and save the money to use during the school year.

Get the Best Jobs on Campus

3. Check into work-study programs at your school. You may be able to find paid work, like an internship, that also counts toward academic credit. The hours for on-campus work-study are usually more flexible than for an off-campus job, which will allow you time for classes and studying.

4. In addition to being flexible, work-study jobs are a good idea for financial aid reasons. Whereas off-campus earnings are included in your income and reported on the Free Application for Student Aid (FAFSA), work-study earnings are not, so you won't be expected to contribute those earnings to the cost of tuition, room, and board.

5. The early bird gets the worm (or in this case, the work) when it comes to applying for on-campus work-study jobs. The best jobs get taken quickly, so apply as soon as you arrive on campus.

6. Landing a part-time job in the student bookstore can score you a hefty discount on your textbooks. If your school offers a 25 percent discount, and the average cost of books for the school year is $1,200, you could save $300 per year on books by taking advantage of the employee discount.

7. If the job listings at the student employment office are scarce by the time you arrive on campus, go directly to the places where you'd be interested in working, like the library, computer center, campus bookstore, or physical education building, and apply directly. Job openings are not always posted in the employment office. If you can't find a job you want right away, keep checking every few weeks.

8. The campus library is a great place to work. You may find time to study while you're on the job, especially if you work evenings or early mornings when things are quiet.

9. Check into becoming a student assistant to one of your professors. You can earn extra cash while gaining valuable experience in your field.

Four Good Off-Campus Jobs

10. Find a job that pays tips, like waiting tables, bartending, delivering pizza, detailing cars at a car wash, or catering. You'll make more per hour than you would at many other jobs, sometimes as much as twice the minimum wage—or better.

11. If you read up on how to make popular mixed drinks, you can earn great tips bartending for local restaurants or caterers. You also get to meet a lot of interesting people, and bartending is a skill you can always fall back on in a pinch.

12. Get a part-time job at a restaurant that provides free staff meals while you're on duty. You'll save a bundle on food. This will only work well if you like the type of food the restaurant serves. For health reasons (and your waistline), it's probably best if it's not a fast-food joint.

13. Work as a caddy at the local golf course. You get to spend time outside, work on your tan, hit a few balls now and then, and earn some money, including tips.

Tips for Being Your Own Boss in College

14. Not interested in committing to a regular job while taking classes? Try earning money with skills you already possess. Think of something you're good at that other students or residents of the town need. Create flyers on your computer and post them around campus and your dorm, offering your services for a fee.

15. One of the easiest ways to make extra cash is to tutor a fellow classmate in one of your best subjects. Just because calculus or French is easy for you doesn't mean it is for everyone else. Tutoring allows you to choose your own work hours and earn a decent hourly rate.

16. Baby-sit for in-town families or for students with kids. Baby-sitting can command a higher hourly rate than you might imagine, so check around and find out what the going rate is in your area. The more kids you baby-sit at one time, the higher the rate. After the little ones are in bed, you'll have quiet time for studying.

17. Get physical. Mow lawns, help with weeding, gardening, or landscaping in summer, and shovel walks and driveways in winter. Busy adults are often willing to pay good money to have someone else do these time-consuming chores.

18. If you have access to a lawnmower, contact area real estate companies and offer your services mowing and maintaining lawns for vacant homes that are for sale. Somebody has to take care of these yards so they look good to prospective buyers, and it might as well be you. Find out the going rate in your area and price your services accordingly.

19. If your family owns enough land to allow you to do some planting, take advantage of the growing season to start your own pumpkin patch and sell pumpkins to the public in the fall. You can offer pick-your-own pumpkins and let the buyers do all the work, or you can harvest them yourself and charge more.

20. If you can get permission from a tree lot owner to trim approximately twelve inches from the ends of balsam tree branches, you can make your own fresh balsam wreaths and sell them during the holiday season. Since trimming is good for the trees, permission should be easy to obtain. The only other supplies necessary (unless you want to offer decorating services) are a metal ring to attach the balsam to and wire to attach it with. You can sell the finished wreaths for anywhere from $10 to $30 each depending on the going price where you live, at a cost to you of approximately $1.50 to $2.00 per wreath.

21. During the holidays, offer gift-wrapping services to local stores, fellow students, or neighbors. Post notices around campus, at grocery store bulletin boards, and other public places. Some smaller stores may allow you to set up a table in the store and wrap presents for customers after they finish shopping.

22. Sign up to be a mystery shopper. Many retailers and restaurants hire college students to pose as customers and observe employee behavior, then report back on the quality of the service. Getting paid to eat or shop: can it get any better?

23. Start your own pet-sitting service. Pet-sit for neighbors on vacation or walk dogs while people are at work. In many cities, vacationers or traveling businesspeople pay $10 or more per visit for someone to come into their home to feed and walk their pet.

24. Detail cars. This is another chore that busy adults are often more than willing to pay someone else to do. All you need is a hose and a water hook-up, a bucket, car cleaner and wax, a sponge, and a few soft cloths. Take the car to a do-it-yourself car wash or clean it in the owners' driveway using their hose and water.

25. Type school papers for other students who don't have the time or whose keyboard skills are not as good as yours. Read local newspaper ads to see what the going rate is and charge a little less than that, either by the page or by the hour.

26. Offer shopping services for busy adults. Learn how to find the best prices online by using some of the price comparison search engines like www.pricegrabber.com. For a flat fee or a percentage of the savings, do the legwork for your customers.

27. If you love music, start a DJ service on campus. You'll need to make an investment in equipment, but you may have some of it already. Expect to earn between $200 and $300 per gig. Use word-of-mouth, business cards you can print from your own computer, flyers around campus, and a listing in the campus phone directory to advertise your service.

28. Clean houses or other students' dorm rooms. Post notices on the bulletin boards of local grocery stores and around campus to find customers. Many businesses also hire college students to clean offices at night.

29. Are you good at troubleshooting Windows or Mac OS computer problems? Do you have a knack for resolving hardware issues? Can you help people get online or set up their modem or wireless Internet connection? Use your expertise to help other students or adults resolve their computer problems and charge a fee that your fellow students can afford.

30. Be a mother's helper or part-time nanny for a busy mom. Place a line ad in the local newspaper or scout the classifieds for these types of jobs near your school. Line ads are inexpensive and even offered as a free service at some newspapers.

31. If you live off campus and have your own yard, plant a garden and sell your produce to neighbors and other students. If you're really ambitious, form a student co-op to manage a joint garden and sell your wares at a local farmers' market. Take a fee off the top for managing the co-op and split the rest of the income with the other participants.

32. If you have access to a kitchen and you like to cook, make baked goods and sell them to neighbors or at a local farmers' market. Homemade breads, cookies, cupcakes, cakes, pies, and other treats are nearly always bestsellers at these events.

33. Come up with creative ways to earn money by assessing the needs you see on campus. Is the nearest grocery store a fifteen-minute walk away? Start an affordable delivery service so students who live on campus don't have to lug heavy groceries back to the dorm. Use your imagination and your powers of observation to come up with other ideas.

34. Buy small antiques or collectibles and auction them on eBay. Leave the more expensive items for someone else to buy and sell, unless you're knowledgeable about their worth. You don't want to be stuck paying more for something than you can get for it.

35. If you're Web savvy and capable of setting up a website that can attract significant traffic, you can make money with affiliate programs. Sign up with sites like Amazon, All Posters, or businesses related to your website topic. You'll earn a commission every time someone makes a purchase after clicking on an affiliate's link on your site.

Four Offbeat Ways to Make Money

36. Volunteer for experiments conducted by your college's psychology department. You'll be paid by the hour or earn a flat fee for each experiment. It's a good way to earn extra cash without a long-term time commitment.

37. Donate plasma to your local blood bank and make $15 to $30 a pop. You must be in good health and drug-free. This isn't a good way to make steady income but it can help get you out of a temporary cash bind.

38. Returning recyclable bottles and cans may seem like a pain in the neck, but the deposit fees can add up. It goes without saying that you should turn in your own recyclables, but you can also offer to dispose of your dormmates' empties and collect the empties after parties in exchange for the bottle deposits. Stash the cash away for an emergency or for an occasional splurge on something you otherwise wouldn't justify spending money on.

39. This moneymaking venture isn't for everyone, but these days, male college students are frequently making donations to sperm banks at around $40 per deposit. It's not exactly a steady job, but it provides a few extra dollars when you really need it.

Other Cash-Generating Ideas

40. Instead of spending the money from birthdays, Christmas and other holidays, work bonuses, tax refunds, and other cash windfalls, save it in your college bank account. It will reduce the amount you need to borrow to get through college and lower your interest expenses.

41. Sell something of value to raise money. Before you leave for school in the fall, go through your closets, garage, basement, and attic to scout for items you or your family no longer use or need. Collectibles like baseball cards, autographed sports paraphernalia, coins, music CDs, or similar items could score you some extra cash.

42. If your parents have any U.S. government savings bonds in their names, now may be a good time to cash them in. If they use the proceeds to pay for qualified education expenses (tuition and fees) for the year in which they cash in the bonds, the income they've earned on them may be tax free. There are a number of restrictions, though. For instance, your parents will get the deduction only to the extent that tuition and fees exceed your financial aid and scholarships; their income must fall below the threshold; and any other tax credits and deductions they take, like the Hope Scholarship Credit and the Tuition deduction, will reduce their income deduction on the savings bonds. See IRS Publication 970 for details.

43. You may have unclaimed money waiting for you to stake a claim. It could be unused gift certificates, life insurance left to you, a balance in a forgotten bank account, a refund owed you, or other funds being held for you. Contact the Unclaimed Property Administrator in your state government or search online at www.uphlc.org (if your state provides information online).

44. Do you have any stocks that you could sell to help pay for college? Ask your parents if they or any other relatives ever bought stocks in your name. If so, consider selling them to help pay tuition or room and board. If you're lucky, a relative may even be willing to sell stocks or mutual funds they own themselves and gift the cash to you for college expenses.

45. Are there any cash-value insurance policies in your name that your parents or grandparents might have taken out for you when you were younger? People often forget they ever bought these old policies. If such a policy exists, consider cashing it in and using the money toward tuition or other college expenses.

46. Sign up to critique ads online for www.brandport.com. You'll be paid for each ad you watch and answer questions about. Depending on how fast you can do it and how many you do, you could earn up to $30 in an hour.

47. Turn your trash into cash by getting rid of stuff you no longer need at a yard sale. Attract more customers by getting other students to join in. You may be able to get permission to hold your sale in a campus facility. Advertise your yard sale on the online campus bulletin board system and look for free classified listings in local newspapers.

48. If you have a big-ticket item to sell, like computer or exercise equipment, try selling it with a classified ad in a newspaper or online. You'll probably get more for it than you would at a yard sale.

49. Used books, CDs, DVDs, and books on tape are popular items for resale. Some stores will pay you cash, while others will give you credit toward new items.

50. Many college students shop at consignment stores, so when you tire of your clothes, don't leave them hanging in your closet, throw them out, or give them away. Place them in a consignment shop and when they sell, the shop owner will pay you a percentage of the sale.

51. Tell your parents about www. upromise.com, where they can register their credit and debit cards and earn money back on purchases they make with their cards. The amounts, which can be used for college expenses, are small, but every little bit helps.

2.

Maximize Your Financial Aid

You've probably read up on Pell grants, work-study, Stafford loans, Alternative loans, and other forms of financial aid until your head hurt, so we won't rehash the basics here. Instead, we'll cover the not-so-well-known tips and tricks for finding financial aid and getting as much mileage out of it as possible, how to make sure you don't disqualify yourself from your financial aid awards, and how to get the U.S. government to help pay for your college education. You'll also learn critical strategies for increasing the amount of financial aid you're eligible to receive.

Understand the Big Picture

52. Give yourself a thorough crash course in financial aid. Read up about it at www.finaid.com so you'll understand the big picture and how the different sources of aid work. With this understanding, you'll be able to take full advantage of everything that's available to you and you won't be kicking yourself later for missing out on sources of potential aid.

53. Talk to your parents early about financial aid. Make sure you're on the same page with them about how much financial support they'll be able to provide for college and what each of you will do to get through the financial aid process and meet all the deadlines. Lack of communication with your parents on this subject could cost you lots of money.

54. Think of your quest for financial aid as a job—one that will pay handsomely. Devote as much time to it as possible. Every dollar in grants or scholarships you receive is a dollar you don't have to borrow and, more importantly, a dollar that won't have years of compounding interest expense added to it.

55. Not only is your quest for financial aid a job, it's one that you'll have for at least four years. Applying for financial aid is a yearly process. If you're serious about finding money for college, you'll be completing forms, writing essays, surfing the Internet looking for scholarships, and talking to guidance counselors and other experts right up until the year you graduate from college.

56. A heads-up about Early Decision. If you choose this route, you'll know whether you've been accepted to the school of your choice by early winter, but you won't know what your financial aid award is until spring. This means you'll have to accept or reject your Early Decision offer without knowing anything about your financial aid package. If your award is not enough and you can't come up with the balance, you may have to attend another school.

57. Complete the financial aid forms and calculate your eligibility before you apply to colleges for admission, even if you don't think you're eligible for financial aid. Applying early improves your chance of receiving the best financial aid package you can. If you apply late and the college has already committed its available financial aid funds for the year, they may not be able to do anything for you until the following year.

58. Use the calculator at the College Board's website (www.collegeboard.com) to calculate what your EFC (expected family contribution) will be. This site also includes numerous other free calculator tools, so take advantage of them.

59. If you're not satisfied with the financial aid package offered by your college of choice, don't despair. You may be able to receive additional funding by explaining your financial circumstances. Contact the financial aid office and be assertive, but not pushy. You'll want these people on your side for the next four years and you don't need a reputation for being a pain in the butt.

60. If a school that's not your top choice offers more financial aid than your first choice, send a copy of the higher award letter to your first choice and ask if there's any possibility of additional aid so you can afford to attend that college. Sometimes if a school sees that you've been offered more aid elsewhere, they'll try to find more funds for you. This works best if the school is eager to have you as a student (because of your scholastic background, athleticism, talent, or other characteristic).

61. Similarly, you can use this strategy to increase your chances of getting a good financial aid package. Apply to schools with similar characteristics (such as average SAT score or average GPA) or where your traits will be above the pack (you are from Nebraska but apply to a school in the Northeast, or you play the trumpet well and the band might need you). That way, if one of the schools offers less financial aid, you might be able to get a school to reconsider your aid package.

62. Don't rule out expensive colleges just because you think you can't afford them. Some schools have large endowments and offer larger financial aid packages than others do. You may end up with the same out-of-pocket costs that you'd incur at a less expensive school, or even lower.

63. Less financial aid is available for part-time students, so if possible maintain a full-time status, even if you have to work. Most schools consider twelve credit hours per semester a full-time load. For most students, this course load is manageable even with a part-time job of up to twenty hours per week.

64. Once you've submitted your financial aid application for your senior year in college (filed during your junior year), you no longer have to worry about your income affecting your eligibility for aid. You can earn as much money as possible during the summer before your senior year and during your senior year without hurting your aid award.

65. When evaluating your out-of-pocket costs of attending one school versus another, you need to be able to compare the total costs minus the financial aid package you are offered. To help you make this comparison, ask the financial aid office of each school what the average financial aid award offered to students is each year. The school you think you can't afford to attend may actually end up being cheaper than the one you thought you had to settle for.

66. Before you get too excited about your financial aid package, read all the fine print to make sure the offer is good for all four years of college. More and more schools are placing expiration clauses in their aid packages, so make sure you know exactly how long the school's commitment extends. Even better, get it in writing.

67. If your financial situation changes significantly after you've been awarded a financial aid package, notify the financial aid office of the change and ask if they'll reconsider your award. Financial changes that may qualify you for additional aid include: drop in family income due to job loss, retirement, or significantly lower earnings; one of your siblings also enrolling in college; high medical costs due to serious illness or hospitalization; death of a parent; or your parents' divorce or legal separation.

68. If you have a sibling who is in college, consider attending the same school. Some colleges provide tuition discounts for families with more than one student in the same college.

69. Ask about the student loan default rate at the schools you're applying to. If the rate is too high, the school will be prohibited from awarding federal financial aid, which could be a nasty surprise that makes the funding of your education much more difficult.

70. Think twice before underreporting your income on your financial aid application. Schools audit a large percentage of applications, and if they discover that your income is more than you reported, you might be required to repay some of the funds you were awarded. If you don't pay up, they may turn your account over to the U.S. Department of Education for collection.

Eleven Tips for Filing Your Financial Aid Applications

71. A recent study revealed that hundreds of thousands of college students who may have been eligible for financial aid didn't get one red cent because they didn't apply. Don't assume you're not eligible for financial aid. Complete and submit the Free Application for Federal Student Aid (FAFSA) forms, regardless of your family's financial situation or whether you're attending a four-year college or a community college.

72. Notice the word "free" in the name of the application used by all U.S. students seeking financial aid: Free Application for Federal Student Aid. If you visit a website that asks for payment to submit the FAFSA, you're not at the official U.S. Department of Education website (www.fafsa.ed.gov). Don't pay for something you can get free.

73. The FAFSA deadline is tricky. The earliest you can file is January 1, because the information is based on the prior calendar year, but you won't have your income tax return completed by then. Submit the FAFSA as soon as possible after the deadline, even if it means you have to estimate your income and expenses; you can always correct them later if necessary. It can take up to six weeks for the form to be processed, and you want to be sure it arrives at the schools you've applied to before they begin awarding financial aid, or you may lose out.

74. Many private colleges and some state schools require the CSS/Financial Aid PROFILE form in addition to the FAFSA. Don't disqualify yourself for aid by failing to file the specific form required by each school. To obtain the PROFILE form, register at the College Board website (www.collegeboard.com). You'll be required to pay a fee, so have a credit card number handy. You can also register via telephone.

75. Some schools require supplemental financial aid forms in addition to the FAFSA and PROFILE form. Read all of the material in the admissions applications of the schools you apply to and determine if any supplemental forms are required. Send these forms (except for the FAFSA or CSS/PROFILE form) directly to the school.

76. Make sure you complete the correct version of the FAFSA. The year on the form should be the academic year for which you're applying for aid (for example, 2005–2006 for the academic year that begins in the fall of 2005). The same applies if you complete the form online. If you use a form with the wrong date, you won't be awarded any financial aid in the year you need it.

77. After you submit information to financial aid offices, follow-up with a phone call or email after a reasonable amount of time to make sure they've received what you sent. If the items didn't reach their destination or are languishing in a pile on someone's desk, a phone call could prevent you from missing out on financial aid.

78. You should also follow-up with a phone call after you submit financial aid information online to ensure that it's been physically received. Don't rely on an email confirmation. By the time a letter from the school notifying you that there's a problem arrives in your mailbox, all the financial aid available for the year may have been awarded to other students.

79. You have to submit a FAFSA every year to be eligible for aid. Write the date on your calendar so you don't miss out on the financial aid awards. After the first year, you may be able to file a renewal FAFSA, which is easier than recreating the entire form. If you don't receive a copy of the renewal FAFSA in the mail, you should be able to get a copy at your school's student financial aid office.

80. Filing your financial aid applications (not the FAFSA) with the schools is like filing your income tax return. To reduce your chances of an audit, experts recommend that you file as close to the deadline as possible. Financial aid officers can't begin awarding aid until the priority-filing deadline, and if your application is sitting around while they're waiting, the officers will have more time to go over your application with a fine-tooth comb and find problems.

81. Filing your FAFSA and other required financial aid forms correctly is critical to your success in obtaining financial aid. To get the inside scoop on all the ins and outs of properly completing the forms, don't miss the Princeton Review's "FAFSA and PROFILE Strategies" on their website at princetonreview.com/college/finance/FAFSA.

82. If you or a parent served in the U.S. military, you may be eligible for education assistance benefits. The U.S. Department of Veteran Affairs provides assistance via the Montgomery GI Bill, Veterans Educational Assistance Program, Survivors' and Dependents' Educational Assistance Program, Work-Study, Tutorial Assistance, and other programs. Call your VA office or your financial aid officer.

83. If you're married, you may also be eligible for veterans' educational benefits if your spouse is a veteran. Call your U.S. Department of Veterans Affairs office or visit www.gibill.va.gov for more information.

84. If you enlist in the U.S. Army or Air Force in certain military occupational specialties, you may be eligible for education benefits under the Montgomery GI Bill, the Army's College Fund, and other programs.

85. The U.S. Public Health Service (part of the U.S. Department of Health and Human Services) offers loans, scholarships, and faculty loan repayment programs to students preparing for a degree in health professions, such as dentistry, optometry, public health, and veterinary medicine.

86. If you become a full-time teacher in an elementary or secondary school serving low-income families, you may qualify to have part of your Perkins Loans forgiven under the National Defense Education Act. Under this program, 15 percent of your Perkins loan is forgiven in the first and second years you teach, 20 percent is forgiven in the third and fourth years, and 30 percent in the fifth year.

87. If you received a Stafford loan after October 1, 1998, and have taught for five years in a low-income school, you may be eligible to have up to $5,000 of your Stafford loan cancelled by the U.S. Department of Education.

88. If you're economically disadvantaged or a dislocated worker, find out if you're eligible for tuition and free job training assistance under the Workforce Investment Act (WIA) administered by the U.S. Department of Labor, or other legislation that assists people in your situation.

89. The Reserve Officers' Training Corps (ROTC) provides one-, two-, and four-year scholarships that cover most of the cost of tuition, books, and fees and provide a monthly allowance. In return, you participate in summer training while you're in college and serve in the military for a specified time after graduation.

90. For information on other recruitment incentives offered by the U.S. Armed Forces, visit the U.S. Department of Defense (DOD) website at www.todaysmilitary.com.

91. If you volunteer for the Peace Corps, you may be able to have your Stafford, Perkins, and Consolidation loans deferred, and your Perkins loans partially cancelled, while helping less fortunate people in one of seventy developing countries. For each year of service, 15 percent of your Perkins loans can be cancelled. Contact the Peace Corps at 1-800-424-8580 or 1-202-692-1845, or visit www.peacecorps.org.

92. Volunteer to serve a year or two in Ameri-Corps, a national service organization that provides education awards of $4,725 in exchange for one year (1,700 hours) of work in community service. The Volunteers in Service to America (VISTA) program provides volunteer opportunities with private, nonprofit groups that help to fight hunger, homelessness, illiteracy, and poverty in the U.S. The AmeriCorps National Civilian Community Corps (NCCC) and AmeriCorps State/National offer similar programs. Call 1-800-942-2677 or 1-202-606-5000, or visit www.americorps.org.

93. Join the Army National Guard full- or part-time while you're in school and earn money for college under one of several programs, such as the 100 percent Federal Tuition Assistance Program, $10,000 for a six- or eight-year enlistment as a member of a unit, help with student loans, or other monetary benefits. Call 1-800-GoGuard or visit www.1800goguard.com/education/education.html for details.

94. Take steps to maximize your eligibility for need-based financial aid. For example, if you (or your parents) have stashed away money that you won't need immediately, consider paying off consumer debt, like credit card balances. Credit card debt is not factored into the financial aid eligibility equation, but assets such as cash are. By depleting your cash balance to pay off debt, you maximize the amount of aid you're eligible for and reduce your interest costs at the same time.

95. You're expected to contribute 35 percent of the assets in your name each year before you're eligible for financial aid. Your parents need only contribute around 6 percent of their assets, so the fewer assets in your name, and the more in your parents' names, the better you'll fare when awarded financial aid. Keep this in mind as you save for college and throughout your college years, and you'll qualify for more aid.

96. Spend your own assets and income before spending those of your parents. Since you're expected to pay a larger percentage of your assets than your parents are, depleting your assets first will increase your eligibility for aid.

97. Your parents should avoid taking disbursements from their retirement account to pay for your education, not only because they're going to need that money for retirement, but also because withdrawals are considered taxable income and will reduce your eligibility for next year's aid. If your parents must tap their retirement funds to pay for your schooling, they should take out loans rather than withdrawals, if possible.

98. You and your parents should plan ahead to avoid incurring capital gains during the years their (or your) income is used to calculate your financial aid (junior year of high school through junior year of college). Capital gains are income for tax purposes, so selling stocks and bonds and incurring capital gains will reduce your eligibility for aid the next year. If you have to sell stocks or bonds in that time frame, offset some of the gain by also selling any stocks or bonds that have lost money.

99. If you're planning to buy a new computer or use some of your savings for another major purchase for college, consider doing it before you complete the financial aid forms. Your savings lowers the amount of financial aid you're eligible for; so spending the money early (on college necessities, of course) will increase your eligibility for aid.

100. Income you earn will reduce your eligibility for financial aid, so talk to your financial aid officer before getting a job during the school year to make sure you won't actually end up worse off. If you have unmet need (if the school was not able to give you enough aid to cover the difference between your estimated family contribution and the cost of attending school), a job makes sense, but don't seek employment without knowing how it will affect your eligibility for financial aid.

101. Although Coverdell Education Savings Accounts can be owned by students or the student's family, financial aid officers consider Coverdells an asset that belongs to you, not your parents. They use a formula that factors in how much money you have in a Coverdell or a state prepaid tuition plan when awarding financial aid. The more you have in these accounts, the less financial aid the school will offer you, so it's to your advantage to tap these sources first when spending for college. Many financial experts recommend cashing in a Coverdell account by December of your senior year in high school so it won't show up as an asset on your financial aid application.

102. If you didn't qualify for financial aid, or received very little, but you now have a sister or brother who is about to enter college, reapply. Families with more than one student in college may qualify for aid that their income previously prevented them from receiving.

Special Financial Aid for Special People

103. If you're deaf, blind, dyslexic, or otherwise disabled, look into special scholarships and financial aid for people with disabilities by searching online using keywords similar to "scholarships disabled." There are numerous scholarship programs specifically for people with disabilities and you may also qualify for state and federal programs. A good reference, which you might find in your local library, is *Financial Aid for the Disabled and Their Families*, by David Weber and Gail Schlachter. The book is updated every two years.

104. Many states provide free tuition at state schools to college-aged children of veterans who were killed or severely disabled during a period of declared war or conflict. You may also be eligible if you're the widow or widower of a veteran or the spouse of a veteran who is missing in action or disabled. Consult your high school guidance counselor, state veterans services office, or your college financial aid office for details on how to apply.

105. A few states provide free tuition at state schools for qualified Native American Indians. The Association on American Indian Affairs also offers scholarships to Native American students who are from a federally recognized tribe and are at least one-quarter Indian blood. For more information, see www.indian-affairs.org/scholarships.cfm.

106. If you're at least sixty-five-years old and can demonstrate financial need, your state may waive your tuition costs if you want to attend a state college as an undergraduate. Contact your state's higher education agency for information.

3.

Maximize Your Scholarships

Every student preparing for college is well aware that the search for scholarships is an important part of funding an education, and many students win at least a few scholarships. Don't be satisfied to stop there. Persistence, hard work, and creativity can generate substantial awards that will greatly reduce your need to borrow money.

107. Your college is an obvious source of potential scholarships, but it pays to be aware of the various types of awards it offers. College awards are often included as part of the overall financial aid package offered to students, along with loans, grants, work-study programs, and other forms of aid. Your college may also award merit-based scholarships for academic achievement, and specific departments within your college may use scholarships to attract or retain students in the department's field of study. Contact your department about the latter type of scholarship, even if you've already been awarded scholarships as part of your financial aid package.

108. Check with your parents' employers to see if they offer any scholarships. Large companies are more likely to have such programs, but some small employers have scholarship funds. Also check with other local businesses, which may award scholarships to local students as a public service and an investment in the community, even if the students have no affiliation with the company. You often have a greater chance of receiving a private corporation award because geographic, employment, and other restrictions limit the number of candidates.

109. If one or both of your parents belongs to a labor union, find out if the union offers scholarships, grants, or low-interest loans to members' college-bound kids. This is a common union benefit, but your parents may be unaware of it. The AFL-CIO website has a searchable database with over four million dollars in union-sponsored scholarships at 66.109.241.150/unionplus/scholarship.html.

110. Read a few books about scholarships, such as *Winning Scholarships for College* by Marianne Ragins, *The Scholarship Book: The Complete Guide to Private-Sector Scholarships, Fellowships, Grants, and Loans for Undergraduates* by Daniel J. Cassidy and Ellen Schneid, *Scholarship Handbook 2005* by Joseph A. Russo, or *The Scholarship Scouting Report: An Insider's Guide to America's Best Scholarships* by Ben Kaplan. The time you invest in this type of research could pay off handsomely in the form of additional awards. You don't have to shell out the cash to buy the books; most libraries have them, or you can sit down with a copy of the book at your local bookstore and take notes.

111. The best way to search for scholarships is the Internet, and with over $1 billion in scholarships listed, the best scholarship search engine is FastWeb (www.fastweb.com). Enter your profile information and you'll receive an email with a list of scholarships you may be eligible to receive, based on your background. You'll also be sent updates when new scholarships for which you're eligible are added to the database. Also search on the Internet using the keywords "financial aid," "student aid," and "scholarships."

112. In addition to FastWeb, you should search some of the other free online scholarship databases, such as those at College Board (apps.collegeboard.com/cbsearch_ss/welcome.jsp), SRN Express (www.srnexpress.com), and Princeton Review (www.princetonreview.com). These are the largest, so it pays to concentrate most of your efforts on them.

113. When searching for sources of financial aid, don't overlook religious organizations, clubs in your city or town, and fraternities or sororities, which often award scholarships or grants to worthy students.

114. Private foundations often award scholarships that may not be highly publicized. Ask the reference librarian at your local library for a directory of local charities and foundations. Also visit www.cof.org/locator for a list of local foundations in your state. Contact them to find out if they award any scholarships.

115. If you're a member of an ethnic group, be sure to look into ethnicity-based organizations, many of which award scholarships. Awards are made to Jewish people, African Americans, American Indians, Pacific Islanders, Hispanics, and many other minorities.

Four Ways to Find Local Scholarships

116. You won't find many local scholarships on the big Internet scholarship search engines, but don't leave local sources of money out of your search. Check with local organizations such as Rotary International, Kiwanis Club, Elks Club, Daughters of the American Revolution (DAR), American Legion, Lions Club, YMCA, and Veterans of Foreign Wars (VFW), which all award scholarships on a local level. Look in the Yellow Pages of your telephone directory or online for the telephone numbers of these organizations.

117. Your guidance counselor is usually the best source of local scholarship information. Most local organizations provide information to high school guidance offices on a regular basis. Another good source is your local library. Ask a librarian for help.

118. Check your local newspapers for announcements of scholarships awarded to local students, and then contact these organizations about how to apply for the next round of scholarships. The newspaper announcements usually occur between March and June, when most scholarships are awarded. You can browse through past issues of newspapers at your local library to find announcements.

119. Contact your local chamber of commerce and ask if they know of any member businesses that award scholarships to area students. Contact those businesses directly and ask how to apply.

120. Some serious scholarship monies are awarded for rather offbeat reasons. One example is the Chick and Sophie Major Memorial Duck Calling Contest in Stuggart, Arkansas, which results in the award of a $1,500 scholarship to a high school student who wins a duck-calling contest by showing proficiency in four calls: hailing, feeding, comeback, and mating calls. Contact the Stuggart, Arkansas, chamber of commerce for information.

121. Another offbeat scholarship is offered by Tall Clubs International (www.tall.org), which awards $1,000 scholarships to members chosen by their local Tall Clubs chapter. Women must be at least 5' 10" tall and men must be at least 6' 2" tall to be considered.

122. Ancestry can even play a part in scholarship awards: Hood College in Frederick, Maryland, has a heritage scholarship that lets incoming freshmen pay the same first-year tuition as their parents or grandparents paid, regardless of the year their ancestor attended.

123. Creative couples that win the "Stuck at the Prom" contest sponsored by Duck Brand Duct Tape each win a $2,500 scholarship for attending their high school prom wearing attire they created out of colorful duct tape. There are three divisions: traditional prom attire, theme/costume wear, and "just plain silver." Visit the "Stuck at the Prom" website at www.duck-tapeclub.com/contests/prom for details.

124. Many other criteria are used for evaluating and granting scholarships. There are awards for transfer students, Eagle Scouts, Model Senate participants, students who create stylish wool garments (National Make it Yourself From Wool Competition), left-handed students (Juniata College's Beckley Scholarship), short people less than 4' 10" (The Little People of America Association), overweight people (The New England Chapter of the National Association to Advance Fat Acceptance), skateboarders with a 2.5 or higher GPA (Patrick Kerr Skateboard Scholarship), covens and wiccans (The Coven of the Sacred Waters), and twins.

125. The Bill and Melinda Gates Foundation funds the Gates Millennium Scholars to provide thousands of outstanding minority students who are economically disadvantaged with an opportunity for a college undergraduate education in any field, or a graduate education in mathematics, science, engineering, education, or library science. For nomination materials, see www.gmsp.org or your high school guidance counselor.

126. If you're a woman considering a career in aeronautics, science, engineering, or business, you may qualify for a scholarship from Zonta International, a global service organization of executives in these fields working across political and social boundaries to advance the status of women worldwide. They also award fellowships. Visit their website at www.zonta.org for details.

127. The Coca-Cola Scholars Foundation awards scholarships each year to 250 U.S. high school seniors with a GPA of at least 3.0 on a 4.0 scale. Fifty National Scholars receive $20,000 and two hundred Regional Scholars receive $4,000 each. Recipients of this highly competitive program are selected based on leadership, character, civic and extracurricular activities, academic excellence, and community service. For more information, call 1-800-306-COKE.

128. The Elks National Foundation awards two renewable (four-year) $15,000 scholarships, two renewable $10,000 scholarships, two renewable $5,000 scholarships, and 494 renewable $1,000 scholarships each year to high school seniors in their Most Valuable Student Competition. Students are scored based on ACT or SAT scores, transcript, employment, extracurricular activities, community service, honors and awards, leadership, recommendations, a counselor report, and an essay. See www.elks.org for details.

129. The Jack Kent Cooke Foundation Undergraduate Transfer Scholarship Program awards the largest scholarships offered in the United States to community college transfer students. Each year, twenty-five students attending community colleges or two-year schools and planning to transfer to four-year institutions are awarded up to $30,000 per year to cover educational expenses for the final two to three years of a baccalaureate degree, including tuition, living expenses, required fees, and books. See www.jackkentcookefoundation.org for details.

130. The Siemens Westinghouse Competition in Math, Science, and Technology results in individual and team regional and national awards to students achieving excellence in science research projects in high school. Regional finalists receive $1,000 each. Regional winners receive $3,000 each and go on to the national competition, where the national individual and team winners receive additional scholarships of $100,000, and runners-up receive $10,000 to $50,000. See www.siemens-foundation.org/competition for details.

131. The Intel Science Talent Search (STS), known as the "Junior Nobel Prize," is America's oldest high school science competition. Each of the three hundred student semifinalists receives a $1,000 award for his or her outstanding original science research. The finalist receives a $100,000 four-year scholarship; the second-place finalist receives a $75,000 scholarship; the third-place finalist receives a $50,000 scholarship; fourth-through sixth-place finalists each receive a $25,000 scholarship; and seventh- through tenth-prize finalists each receive a $20,000 scholarship. See www.intel.com/education/sts for details.

132. Many other nationally coveted scholarships are awarded each year, including those sponsored by various government agencies, associations, foundations, and private corporations. See scholarships.fatomei.com for a listing of many such scholarship programs.

133. Over one billion dollars in athletic scholarships are awarded each year to more than 126,000 student athletes, but the awards are highly competitive. If you think you may qualify for an athletic scholarship, increase your chances of success by learning about the process at www.collegesportsscholarships.com; visit the National Collegiate Athletic Association (NCAA)'s website at www.ncaa.org for details on athletic scholarships; and read the book *The Sports Scholarships Insider's Guide: Getting Money for College at Any Division* by Dion Wheeler.

Thirteen Tips for Winning Scholarships

134. The time to start looking for scholarships is in your junior year of high school. Good grades, wide interests, involvement in extracurricular activities and community affairs, and a skill (sports or music, for example) help you stand out above the crowd when it comes time to award scholarships. Self-marketing skills are an added bonus.

135. Most scholarship deadlines occur during the fall and winter of your senior year, the same time that college admissions and financial aid applications have to be submitted. Plan ahead and begin your scholarship search early so you can spend the summer before your senior year writing essays and completing scholarship applications.

136. When writing essays for scholarships, first acquaint yourself with the ideals of the organization you're applying to, then emphasize your own traits that reflect those same ideals. This technique could give you an edge with the judges, who naturally would love to award a scholarship to a student with ideals shared by the organization itself.

137. If your state lottery had a huge jackpot, you wouldn't buy just one lottery ticket, would you? You shouldn't limit yourself to just a few scholarship applications either. Scholarships are like a huge lottery, except you have the power to influence the outcome. The more scholarships you apply for, the better your chances of winning substantial sums.

138. It may seem like scholarships are a Catch-22. The more of them you're awarded, the more the school reduces your financial aid package. Here's a way to reduce the damage: Meet with the financial aid officer of your college to explain your situation and ask to have the loan portion of your package reduced and leave the grants intact. This reduces the amount you have to repay and you get to keep the free scholarship money.

139. You don't have to be a straight-A student to qualify for a scholarship. Several states offer scholarships to B students from lottery proceeds or other state funds. To keep these scholarships, you have to maintain a B average or better.

140. The National Association of Student Financial Aid Administrators estimates that 350,000 people are cheated out of $5 million in scholarship scams each year. One popular scam is a free seminar about scholarships where you're pressured into signing contracts for hundreds of dollars for "professional" help. At best, you may be provided information you could have obtained free; at worst, you may never hear from the "professionals" once you pay their fee. Some legitimate companies do charge a fee for scholarship information, but they never guarantee scholarships or grants.

141. Another scam that many students or their families fall victim to is providing bank account or credit card information in order to hold a "guaranteed" scholarship that you're told you qualify for. The scam artists use this information to debit money from your bank account or make unauthorized charges to your credit card. No legitimate scholarship service will request bank account or credit card information.

142. As you advance in your education, there are more opportunities for academic and career-related scholarships that you wouldn't have been eligible for in your first year or two of college. Check with your school's financial aid office and the academic department for your major regularly about scholarship opportunities specifically for students in your field of study.

143. Many organizations and colleges offer scholarship money based at least in part on geography. For example, in an effort to foster interest in technology, some professional chapters of the National Technical Association award scholarships to local students in their geographical area who are majoring in science and engineering fields. Another example is the College Foundation of North Carolina, which awards scholarships to children or grandchildren of Vietnam veterans living in certain counties in North Carolina.

144. Ethnicity is another criteria used in many awards. The Ford Foundation Postdoctoral Fellowships for Minorities awards substantial fellowships to Native Americans, Alaskan Natives, African Americans, Mexican Americans, Native Pacific Islanders, and Puerto Ricans engaged in or planning a teaching and research career. The American Sociological Association awards scholarships to minority students studying sociology. Hispanic Designers Scholarships gives awards to Hispanic American students with a minimum GPA of 2.5 who pursue design-related fields. Search for scholarships that may be given for any criteria you meet, whether it's based on location, ethnicity, interests, skills, ancestry, or anything else.

145. Concentrate primarily on local scholarships even if the amounts are smaller, because there's less competition and your chances of winning are greater. A few small local scholarships can quickly add up to as much, if not more, than one large national scholarship.

146. If you or your friends have older siblings who've already been to college, pick their brains about how to get scholarships, how to write winning essays, and how to avoid pitfalls. You might as well learn from somebody else's mistakes and successes.

147. Read the small print in all of your scholarships and know the requirements you must meet to continue to qualify. For example, many scholarships require that you maintain a certain GPA. There also may be other less obvious requirements. Make sure you know what they are or you could inadvertently disqualify yourself.

148. If you have a scholarship based on playing a particular sport or musical instrument, don't quit that activity mid-semester or you may find yourself repaying the scholarship money you've already spent. Try to tough it out long enough to get as much of the financial benefit as possible.

149. If you have financial aid based on need, you could disqualify yourself if your income exceeds the limits. Check with your financial aid office early in the year to find out how much you can earn without affecting your eligibility, then keep an eye on your income during the year to make sure you don't exceed this amount.

150. If your scholarship is based on majoring in a particular subject and you're contemplating a switch in majors, find out what impact that will have on your scholarship so you can plan accordingly. Will you lose the scholarship? Will you have to repay what you've already received?

151. For multiyear scholarship awards, find out whether it's necessary to complete paperwork each year or if the award automatically renews on an annual basis. Don't risk losing your award by failing to file required paperwork or meet other criteria.

152. If you've received financial aid and you decide to withdraw from classes, consult your financial aid office first. You may have to repay a prorated portion of the financial aid you received if you withdraw before you've completed at least 60 percent of the period for which the funds were given. Some advance planning could save you a significant sum.

153. Before planning to move off campus, check with your financial aid office. Some financial aid packages require you to live on campus. It could be disastrous if you move off campus only to find that you've disqualified yourself from your financial aid.

4.

Understand and Control Credit Card Use

Having your own credit card may seem like a passport to adulthood, but it can also be a one-way ticket to a life of debt. Using credit as a tool instead of a crutch is not as simple as plopping your plastic down on the counter when making a purchase. It's critical to have a thorough understanding of the complexities of using credit cards so you can make smart decisions that will save you from painful mistakes and protect you from becoming a victim of identity theft. Like anything else, the best way to gain that understanding is to research, read, and educate yourself.

154. It's important to understand credit reports, which contain information about where you work and live, whether you pay your bills on time, and whether you've been sued, arrested, or have filed for bankruptcy. The three major credit bureaus—Equifax, Experian, and TransUnion—gather this information from your creditors and sell it to lenders, employers, insurers, and other businesses. Develop an understanding of how credit scores work by reading the explanation at www.myfico.com.

155. Every financial transaction you make could potentially be reported to a credit bureau and find its way onto your credit report. Do everything in your power to prevent black marks that will cost you money. Insurance companies use your credit report to price your insurance premiums; credit card companies, mortgage companies, and other lenders use your credit report to decide whether to lend you money and at what interest rate; landlords use your credit report to decide whether to rent to you; utilities and others use your credit report to decide whether to require a large deposit; and employers use your credit report to decide whether to offer you a job. You get the idea.

156. The Fair Isaac Corporation (FICO) develops your credit, or FICO score, a computer-generated number that is based on all the information in your credit report. This score will determine how much of a credit risk you are. Developing and maintaining a healthy credit score should be one of your top priorities because it will affect every aspect of your financial life.

157. The most important feature of a credit card is the Annual Percentage Rate (APR), which is the interest rate you'd pay on your balance in a twelve-month period. This rate is actually divided by twelve and the resulting rate is applied to your balance each month. If you carry a balance on your card, it's much more important to shop for the card with the best APR than to get perks like frequent flyer miles.

158. Don't fall for the common misconception that you always have a twenty-five-day grace period before you incur interest on your credit card balance. The grace period applies only when you pay your bill off totally and have a zero balance. When you don't pay off the balance every month, you incur interest starting on the day you charge the item to your credit card. Some cards have no grace period even if you pay the balance in full each month.

159. Research the best credit card deals online at a site like www.bankrate.com. You can compare interest rates, grace periods, perks, and annual fees and find the best credit card deals in the country with a few clicks of your mouse. Getting a good credit card deal could save you lots of money over the years.

160. If you find yourself in over your head with credit card debt, don't look to bankruptcy as an answer to your problems. You've danced the dance and it's your responsibility to pay the piper. Bankruptcy has long-term repercussions that could make your life miserable. File for bankruptcy and your insurance rates will go up; you'll have trouble getting a car loan, mortgage, or other loan; you may be unable to rent an apartment; and you may not be able to find a good job.

Good and Bad Things about Credit Cards

161. Use credit cards to help you establish a credit history, which will be important to you when you graduate and are on your own in the "real" world. Be sure that the history you establish is a good one, because credit mistakes you make in college will follow you around for at least seven years on your credit report.

162. Credit cards provide a sense of security from knowing you'll have funds available to you in the event of an emergency, but the temptation to use them as an extension of your income is especially strong in college. If you can't resist using credit for things you can't afford to pay off at the end of the month, put the card away in a safe place to use only for true emergencies.

163. Credit cards provide a monthly overview of your purchases on one statement (assuming you have only one card). The statement provides a simple way to update your monthly budget. It's much easier than rummaging through a bunch of receipts every month to record your purchases and analyze your spending.

164. Credit cards can be a great tool, but used improperly, they quickly lead to burdensome debt, financial crisis, and possibly bankruptcy. Avoid the expense of high interest rates and compounding interest expense by learning about responsible credit card use before you start using a credit card. See Nellie Mae's Credit Card Tips at www.nelliemae.com/managingmoney/cc_tips.html, or the How Stuff Works tutorial on all things credit at http://money.howstuffworks.com/credit-card.htm for an overview of the ins and outs of credit cards, or read the *Real U Guide to Bank Accounts and Credit Cards* by personal finance columnist and author Ilyce Glink.

165. Surprisingly, more students drop out of college due to unmanageable credit card debt than to academic failure. To make sure this doesn't happen to you, use credit responsibly and avoid charging more than you're sure you can afford to pay off at the end of each month.

166. Leaving college with credit card debt is a drag, because it prevents you from having a better lifestyle after you graduate. Most students have to make sacrifices while in college. If you don't, you'll most likely be making them after you graduate because so much of your income will go toward paying off debt you incurred in college.

167. When you incur debt, you're actually spending your future earnings. This is financial slavery. Paying for an education is considered "good" debt, but to make your life easier after you graduate, it's important to make wise decisions about incurring debt in college. Limit high interest credit card debt and manage all of your financial affairs so you use only as much student loan money as absolutely necessary.

168. A smart card is an alternative to a credit card. It looks like a credit card, but contains a small computer chip with a built in, preset value. Each time you use the card, your purchase is subtracted from the balance, which makes it more difficult to get into trouble. Use a smart card as your first credit card to help you learn to use credit responsibly.

169. Another way to get accustomed to using credit and paying bills on a regular basis without the temptation to get into deep credit card debt is to start off with a secured credit card. These cards are guaranteed by money you deposit in a bank account, so you can never charge more than the money you have designated and set aside in this special account.

170. A prepaid debit card, which allows you to make purchases on the Internet without a credit card, is another alternative to a credit card. Purchases are subtracted from your balance. When you run out, you can reload the card and continue using it.

171. Your best credit card strategy is to have one card with a low interest rate and a low credit limit ($500), use it sparingly, and pay it off every month. This will serve your goals of building a healthy credit history and having funds available for emergencies without the temptation to indulge in uncontrolled spending.

172. Using your credit card to pay for things you know you can afford is the smart way to use credit. It's convenient and helps you build your credit history, and that's a good thing. Using credit as an extension of your income, to pay for things you can't really afford, increases debt, and that's a bad thing. Keeping these concepts in mind can help you control the urge to buy things you can't really afford.

173. Credit cards are not extra income or money available to you to spend. They're loans that you have to pay back, with interest, which means that everything you buy with your credit card ends up costing you more than the purchase price. The longer you take to pay the balance, the more your purchases cost and the less money you have available to spend on other things. For a little reality check, get in the habit of calling your credit card a "loan card," and when you're tempted to use it, ask yourself if you're willing to take out a loan with high interest in order to have the item you're thinking of buying.

174. Ignore the credit card sign-up tables on campus. Don't be tempted by offers of "free" goods like CDs, T-shirts, giant bags of M&Ms, or other cheap trinkets. These sign-up incentives are not really free if you sign up for a credit card with an annual fee or a higher than necessary interest rate just to get the "free" gift.

175. Keep an emergency fund of $500 in a savings account so you won't feel forced to use your credit card when an unexpected expense comes up. Your emergency fund will also provide peace of mind and reduce your money-related stress. If you have to use your emergency fund in a pinch, build it back up as soon as possible.

176. If you can't afford to keep a cash emergency fund, leave enough credit available on your credit card to cover emergencies or unplanned needs like medical expenses or car repairs. Having this cushion for emergencies is one of the main reasons for having a credit card in the first place.

177. Don't sign up for credit cards just so your friend or roommate can get a commission or points from the credit card company by recommending you. Friends don't encourage friends to get into debt. You should make credit card decisions by weighing all the card details in light of how you plan to use the card, and choose the deal that makes the most sense for you.

178. Start off slowly with credit cards. You may be surprised at how difficult it can be to control your spending once you're on your own, away from the influence of your parents. Start out with a $500 line of credit and resolve to pay it off every month. After a semester, if you've stuck with your commitment, raise the credit limit to $1,000 if you feel you need to.

179. Buying on credit can be as addictive as drugs, alcohol, or gambling. As with habit-forming drugs, the best advice is not to get started. Use your card a couple of times a month for necessities only, and pay the balance in full each month. This lets you develop a habit of using credit responsibly and build a healthy credit history.

180. Leave your credit cards at home. Carrying them around with you while you're at the mall or near other temptations is asking for trouble. It's much too easy to buy something you don't really need and may regret buying before you even get home.

181. Never pay for groceries or toiletries with your credit card. If for some reason you can't pay off your balance in full at the end of the month, you'll end up paying interest expense on your food and expendable supplies. Charging day-to-day necessities to your card and not paying the balance in full each month is one of the early warning signs of credit card trouble.

182. Instead of using credit, which spends future resources, set priorities and make informed choices about what's important now versus what's important later, what you want versus what you need, what is ideal versus what is adequate. This is a characteristic of responsible adulthood.

183. Thinking that you need another credit card when you already have one is one of the warning signs that you have a credit problem. Credit cards are not something you collect, like baseball cards. Stop and reevaluate your spending and use of credit. If you really need additional credit, consider increasing the limit on your existing card rather than getting an additional credit card.

184. Don't pay for spring break with your credit card. You may find that you can't afford the minimum payments when you get back. You'd have to pay nearly $150 a month in order to pay off a $1,500 spring break tab in twelve months, at 18 percent interest. Figure out how much you can afford to spend on spring break, divide it by the number of months between now and then, and save that amount each month so you can pay cash when the time comes.

185. When you go out for dinner or drinks with friends, don't collect the cash from your friends and volunteer to put the tab on your credit card, even if it will increase your frequent flier miles or cash-back rewards. The cash will be long gone by the time your credit card statement arrives, and if you can't pay the whole tab, you'll be paying interest not only on your own meal, but on your friends' meals as well.

186. Use credit cards as an absolute last resort for paying college expenses. The average graduate student in 2003 had credit card debt of $7,831, which would take 29 years to pay off at a monthly minimum payment of 2.5 percent and current average interest rates. Your total interest payment would be over $11,000 in addition to the $7,831 you borrowed. Ouch!

187. One problem with credit cards is that you lose sight of the real cost of the items you purchase. Did you think that stereo you bought cost $700? Think again. If you're paying 18 percent interest and it took you a year to pay off the stereo, it really cost you $826. Remember, if you don't pay off your credit card each month, everything you buy costs more.

188. Get in touch with your feelings when you use your credit card. Do you feel important, powerful, euphoric, reckless, or happy? To be in the driver's seat when it comes to using credit, you can't allow your credit card to be a substitute for legitimate things that make you feel good.

189. To keep your credit card purchases within your budget, record each credit card purchase in your check register as though you had written a check. This helps you see at a glance when you've reached the limit that you can afford to pay off at the end of the month and keeps you from getting in over your head.

190. Your first credit card should have a low credit limit of $500. If the credit card company issues you a card with a higher limit, call the number on your statement and ask them to lower it. A low credit limit will act as a safety valve to help you limit your spending until you have time to determine what your spending habits are and whether you'll have trouble handling credit now that you're on your own.

191. Another reason to limit your credit card balances while in college is that once you graduate, you'll also have student loans to pay off. You may not be able to afford both the student loan payments and your credit card payments.

192. If you receive a letter from your credit card company saying they've raised your credit limit, call them and decline the offer. Higher limits are an invitation to spend more than you can afford, and they affect your credit worthiness if you need to borrow for something else, like a car.

193. Credit card companies hand out credit cards to college students like they were candy, but once you graduate, you'll have to earn them by using credit responsibly. Use your college years to build an excellent history of using and repaying credit. Not only will you graduate with little or no credit card debt, you'll also make it easier to get car loans, mortgages, and favorable interest rates.

194. If your credit card balances are high in relation to your income when you graduate from college and are living in the "real" world, the credit card companies will jack up your interest rates. If you thought it was difficult to pay off your balances when the rate was 14 to 16 percent, you will really be hurting when you're paying 24 to 27 percent. You may find it impossible to make even the minimum payments. Keep your credit card balance to a minimum so you don't have to contend with this problem when you graduate.

195. Your credit card debt can also affect the interest rates for privately funded student loans. If you'll need student loans throughout your years of college, keep this in mind and keep a low credit card balance.

Strategies for Controlling Credit Card Use

196. To remind yourself that credit card purchases are loans that you'll have to repay, with interest, write up a sticky note reminder and place it on your credit card. Each time you're tempted to use your credit card, you'll see the reminder, and it might slow you down just enough to think twice.

197. Keep your credit card at home in a safe place. Carrying it with you will encourage you to buy things you can't afford and don't really need. If you have to go back to the dorm to get your card, it gives you a cooling-off period to reconsider whether you really need the item you're tempted to purchase.

198. If there's a discretionary item you feel you must have, like a DVD player or a new electronics game, instead of whipping out the plastic, put away some money every week until you have enough to pay cash for the item. You'll appreciate the item more and you'll save money in the long run by not paying interest.

199. If you can eat it, wear it, or listen to it, you shouldn't charge it on your credit card. Do you really want to be paying off your pizza tab (with interest) five or ten years after graduation?

200. Be aware that people spend more when they use plastic than they do when they use cash. Studies show that people who pay with a credit card don't feel like they're spending "real" money. There can also be a feeling of euphoria when you pay with plastic, but it will be more than offset by the dreariness of paying the balance off, with interest, over a long period of time.

201. According to student loan provider Nellie Mae, the average student graduates from college with six credit cards. Don't be one of them. Having multiple cards looks bad on your credit report and encourages you to buy things you can't afford. Choose one card (the one with the best interest rate and lowest annual fee) and stick with it.

202. When you're tempted to use your credit card, think ahead to after graduation when you're trying to land that dream job. You may give all the right answers in your interviews, but you may not get the job because your potential employer's check of your credit history revealed you were irresponsible in handling your money. Employers may be reluctant to hire you because they fear that financial irresponsibility will spill over into other areas of your life.

203. To make you think twice before whipping out your credit card, put this note on your card or post it where you'll look at it every day: "It would take 61 years to pay off a $5,000 credit card balance if you made the minimum payment each month (assuming a 14 percent interest rate and a minimum payment of 1.5 percent of your balance). In that time, you would pay $16,000 in interest in addition to the $5,000 you borrowed."

5.

How to Be Smart and Safe about Credit Card Debt

Credit cards seem simple: you pay for your purchases with a piece of plastic and when the bill comes you pay as much or as little of it as you want. The truth is that credit cards are very complex; they only seem simple when you don't understand all their intricacies and the implications of how you use them. By boning up on this information before you start using credit, you can save yourself a lot of grief and a lot of money.

204. A fixed-rate card is not really a fixed-rate card. Legally, the credit card company can jack up your interest rate even on a "fixed-rate" card as long as it informs you fifteen days in advance, so there's no guarantee the rate will stay fixed for any longer than that. Read the notices that come with your monthly statement to make sure you don't miss a rate change announcement. This will give you time to shop around for a new card with a better rate if your credit card company announces an increase.

205. The blank checks your credit card company occasionally sends you to use at any business that accepts your credit card come with an outrageously high interest rate. What's worse, most credit card companies apply your payments to your regular balance until it's at zero before they apply even one penny to the balance you incurred from using the blank checks with the higher rate. That means if you always carry a balance on your credit card, you could still be paying higher interest rates on the funds from the check fifteen years from now. The checks are also easy targets for theft, so shred them as soon as you receive them and toss them in the trash.

206. Those "skip a month's payment" notices you get from your credit card company because you've been such a good customer are not really a favor. You'll continue to accrue interest during the "free" month and will end up paying more interest than if you had made your regular monthly payment. Try to resist these tempting offers to skip payments.

207. Typical monthly minimum credit card payments are approximately 90 percent interest (income to the lender), and only 10 percent principal (reducing what you owe). Low minimum payments are not a favor the credit card company provides because they like you. They'll enslave you to the credit card company for the rest of your life, so always pay more than the minimum.

208. Zero percent interest credit card offers are a sales ploy. The interest rate will go up, and may be higher than the rate on a card that doesn't offer zero percent for an introductory period. Read the fine print to make sure you know exactly when the introductory rate expires, and take the offer only if you're positive you can pay off the balance before that date.

209. Cash advances on your credit card are an expensive way to borrow money. Besides the one-time fee of 2 to 4 percent of the amount of the cash advance, the interest rate is usually 2 to 6 percent higher on cash advances than on credit card purchases. In addition, there's usually no grace period on cash advances, so interest begins to accrue immediately.

210. Premium credit cards, like Gold and Platinum cards, are often not worth the additional fees you pay for them. In return for an annual fee that is two to three times that of a standard card, plus higher interest rates, the benefits you receive (discounts, cash back, travel upgrades, special insurance, or some other perk) are often worth less than what you paid for the "privilege" of having the card. These color descriptions appeal to your need for status but they do very little for you financially. A regular card without the fancy-sounding name is usually the best choice for students who carry a balance.

211. Credit card companies offer cobranded affinity cards that contain the name and logo of your school, your favorite sports team, or charitable organization in return for providing commissions (kickbacks) to the organization. Don't consider the cobranding in your decision about which credit card is best for you; look only at the financial considerations. It doesn't make sense to pay higher interest rates or higher fees just to have a name or logo on a credit card you hide away in your wallet. Even though you receive perks, the money comes out of your pocket in one way or another.

212. As of 2003, the average credit card debt for undergraduate students was $3,262. Making the minimum monthly payment of $81 at 18 percent interest, it will take more than twenty-two years to pay off the balance if you never charge another penny. By the time you pay it off, you will have repaid more than double what you borrowed. Does this make sense to a smart college student like you?

213. The credit card companies that line up on campus to hand out credit card applications aren't there because they want to do you a favor by issuing you a credit card even though you may not have a job. They are there because having you and your fellow students committed to them at a young age is worth the millions of dollars in fees they pay your college, at your expense, to set up camp in the places where you hang out. Many colleges also get a percentage of every dollar you ever spend on credit cards you signed up for on campus.

214. If you carry a balance on your credit card, rewards cards like cash back or frequent flyer miles may cost you more than you'll gain in benefits because these cards have higher interest rates. Sign up for a rewards card only if you've proven your ability to pay off your balance every month, and consider the perks as a reward for your good behavior.

215. Think about why a credit card company would give a credit card to someone with no job and no (or very little) income. Either they think your parents will bail you out if you get into debt, or they think you'll become enslaved to credit card debt while you're young and inexperienced and they'll own you for life. Make them wrong on both counts. You'll graduate far ahead of your peers financially if you stay out of credit card debt.

216. If you're looking for a credit card, try to find one without an annual fee. If you already have a credit card with an annual fee, call the phone number on your monthly statement and ask if they'll waive it. Many credit card companies will do so if asked because the credit card industry is very competitive and they want to keep you as a customer.

217. The worst thing about credit card debt is that you can end up paying interest on your interest. As your interest charges accumulate and get rolled into your balance, your next month's interest is calculated on the amount you borrowed, plus the interest you've incurred, creating a snowball effect. That's why it's so important to pay as much as you can and not charge things you can't afford to pay off by the end of the month.

218. Big Brother is watching. A late payment on one credit card will raise your interest rates on all your other credit cards and may raise your car insurance premiums as well. Credit card companies keep a close eye on your credit history. A late payment makes you a higher risk, and people who are higher risks pay higher rates.

219. Never look at just the monthly payment to determine if you can afford a new purchase, whether it's a $100 electronic item or a $20,000 car. Look at the total amount you'll pay in principal and interest over the life of the loan. Almost any amount can be made to look good by stretching out the repayment period, but you're too smart to fall for that gimmick. The longer the repayment period, the more you'll end up paying for your purchase, because of interest.

220. Consider a prepaid credit card as a set of credit training wheels until you have a little practice using credit and are confident that you won't take any nasty spills. You or your parents will set a dollar limit and make a prepayment. You'll be able to monitor your expenditures online or via monthly statements. When your account gets low, you just add more money to your card.

221. Read the fine print—always! Most credit cards have an introductory interest rate, which will most likely go up after a (usually brief) period of time. If you run up charges on your card, you may find yourself unable to make the payments when the rate increases.

222. If you can't pay your credit card balance off at the end of every month, at least find one with a low interest rate. Check the fine print to make sure the low introductory rate lasts more than a few months or you could quickly end up worse off than you started.

223. Avoid department store credit cards like the plague, even if they offer a tempting 20 percent off on your first purchase. Their interest rates are usually double the rates on major credit cards, so stick with issuers like Master Card, Visa, Discover, or American Express, which are accepted nearly everywhere.

224. Don't fall into the trap of thinking you can afford to use your credit card just because you can manage the minimum monthly payment. Most of the minimum payment goes toward interest and very little toward paying off the principal, which means it could take you 20 to 30 years to pay off your balance.

225. Always pay more than the minimum payment on your credit cards, which is usually 2 to 3 percent of your balance. If you pay the minimum payment every month and continue to use your card, you'll literally be paying off the balance for the rest of your life, with high interest costs added in.

226. Frequent flier miles are a big incentive to use one particular credit card, but banks don't offer frequent flier miles out of the goodness of their hearts; they make money on these cards. The interest rates are often several percentage points higher than regular cards, so if you carry a balance it could cost you more than the value of the miles you're earning.

227. Don't accept offers for credit insurance, which covers your credit card payments if you're too ill to work. It usually covers only your minimum payment, and the cost can be high as your credit card balance goes up. You'd be better off using the money to pay down your balance each month.

228. Don't use your cell phone to place credit card orders. Cell phones are not secure, and someone could intercept your phone call and use your credit card number to run up charges. Find a landline where you can order without being overheard.

229. Never, ever take cash advances on your credit card except in a dire emergency (this does not include a big sale on your favorite jeans or the latest electronic gadget). Cash advances come with a hefty price tag: exorbitantly higher interest rates and high fees. The interest at the higher rate accumulates so quickly it may be difficult to pay it off. Many credit card companies apply your payments to your purchases first until you have a zero balance before crediting anything to the cash advance, so you continue to accumulate interest on the cash advance at the higher rate indefinitely.

230. Late payments are costly. If you pay your credit card bill even one day late, not only will you be slapped with a late payment fee of $25 to $39, but your interest rate will be jacked up too. Mark your credit card payment due dates on your calendar or use whatever method works for you to ensure that you send your payment in early enough to be processed and credited to your account before the due date.

231. The easiest way to make sure you pay off your credit card is to sign up for automatic payments. You can choose to have your minimum payment, the complete balance, or any other amount you would like drafted from your checking or savings account each month. This is a responsible way to pay your credit card bill because you have to plan ahead to have enough money in your account to cover the automatic draft. Talk to a customer service person at your bank if you have any questions.

232. Every time you move, even if it's temporary, notify your creditors immediately of your change of address. If bills take longer to get to you or don't get to you at all because your address is incorrect, you'll incur late fees and possible penalties. Even though the post office will forward your mail for a limited time period, it may be delayed enough to make you miss your due date and incur a fee.

233. If you exceed the credit limit on your credit card, you'll be hit with an over-the-limit fee. Unless you pay your balance down before your next statement, you'll be hit with another over-the-limit fee every month until your balance falls below your limit. What a waste of money! When calculating how much credit you have available, don't forget to include an allowance for the interest expense that will be added to your balance at the end of your billing cycle.

234. If you're not satisfied with the quality of an item you purchased with your credit card, notify the credit card company immediately. You don't have to pay for the item until the credit card company investigates your complaint.

235. The "rule of 72" tells us that 72 divided by the interest rate equals the number of years it will take your debt to double. If you have $5,000 of credit card debt at 10 percent interest, your debt will double in 7.2 years (72/10). If the interest rate is 19 percent, your debt will double in just 3.8 years (72/19). This is why you'll never get out of debt if you just pay the minimum balance.

236. If you have more than one credit card and some cards have higher interest rates than others, try to consolidate to a card with a lower interest rate. More of your payments will go toward paying off your debt instead of fattening the coffers of your credit card company.

237. If you want to transfer your credit card balance to a card with a lower interest rate, read the fine print first. Most cards come with a low introductory interest rate that expires in several months. Make sure the rate after that period is not going to be higher than the rate you already have, or you'll end up incurring higher interest costs and owing more.

238. Another reason to read the fine print before transferring your balance to a new credit card: there may be a fee for transferring, usually equal to a certain percent of your balance (5 percent for example). If your balance is $2,000, the fee could be $100 just to transfer. You might be better off applying that money to the balance of your current card.

239. If you have more than one credit card and you're trying to pay one of them off, pay the minimum payment on all but the one with the highest interest rate. On that one, pay as much as you possibly can. This method saves you the most money in the long run because you pay down the balance with the highest interest rate first. This is the only time you should ever pay just the minimum payment on any credit card.

240. If you have more than one credit card, know your statement closing date on each card. When making a purchase, use the card whose statement closing date has most recently passed. This will give you the full use of your grace period to pay for the purchase. However, don't use this technique if you have no grace period and interest is charged from the date of purchase, or it will cost you more instead of less.

241. If you mail your credit card statement one or two days before it's due, expect to be charged a late fee of $25 to $39. To ensure your payment is credited before the due date, allow a minimum of five but preferably seven days before the due date.

242. You know how compound interest works with your savings account (the bank pays you interest on your principal plus interest on the interest the principal has earned). Compound interest works the same way on your credit card, but not in your favor. You pay interest on the amount you borrowed plus interest on the interest if you pay only the minimum payment, so always pay more.

243. When comparing credit cards, check not only the APR (Annual Percentage Rate of interest), but also the grace period. Some cards have little or no grace period, which means you'll pay interest on your balance for a longer period of time each month, resulting in higher costs to you.

244. When comparing credit card deals, look for the following: the best regular (not introductory) rate, no annual fee, a grace period of at least 25 days, and late fees no higher than $20. If you plan well and always pay your bill on time, you won't have to worry about the late fees. A few percentage points in the interest rate can cost you substantially if you carry a balance of more than a few hundred dollars.

245. Use a check card instead of cash or credit for your day-to-day expenses. Cash can easily be lost or stolen, whereas check cards usually offer some protection from fraudulent use if you report their loss or theft immediately. Check cards also enable you to review your expenditures online, making it easier for you to track your expenses and know where your money is going.

246. After you've had your credit card for a year or so, call your credit card company and ask for a lower interest rate. Competition for cardholders is fierce, so your credit card company wants to keep you as a customer (assuming, of course, that you pay your bills).

247. Always check your credit card or other statement as soon as you receive it. Compare each charge to your receipts and verify that the amounts are correct. Make notes of any payments you've made or credits you're expecting and make sure they appear on the bill when they should.

248. If you have bad credit, you'll be an ideal candidate for car dealer scams. You'll be told you must purchase credit life insurance or an expensive extended warranty in order to qualify for a car loan. Familiarize yourself with popular car dealer scams at www.carbuyingtips.com so you can protect yourself.

249. If the due date of your credit card bill doesn't coincide with the dates you get paid, call the credit card company and ask them to change your due date. You'll avoid the expense of chronic late fees, which add up very quickly.

250. Understanding the difference between charge cards and credit cards can save you money. Charge cards give you the convenience of paying for your purchases without cash, but require you to pay the balance in full each month. Credit cards offer revolving credit. As you pay for the credit you've used, it automatically becomes available to you again. The interest charge on any balance you don't pay by the due date is the cost to you.

251. The fewer credit cards you have, the easier your bill paying will be each month and the easier it will be to track your expenses. One card equals one bill. Having three to five credit card bills each month, all due at different times, is asking for trouble. At some point you're sure to miss a payment and get hit with a whopping late charge.

252. If you have trouble obtaining a credit card because you've had bad credit in the past, consider a secured credit card. These cards require a deposit or are tied to a bank account in which you've deposited an amount of money equal to your credit limit on the card. Fees and interest rates are usually higher on secured cards, but they can help you rebuild your good credit.

253. The credit card with the lowest interest rate is the best deal, right? Not necessarily. Look at the overall costs and how you'll use the card. For example, if you're going to pay the balance off each month, the interest rate is less important than the annual fee.

254. According to a survey by Bankrate, the average interest rate of college students' credit cards was 17.66 percent for purchases and 19.67 percent for cash advances, at a time when the average credit card rate in general was 8 percent. Don't make the mistake of signing up for credit cards with these exorbitant rates.

255. The credit card companies' offer of free phone cards or other "free gifts" is a lure to get you hooked on credit. Don't sell yourself so cheaply.

256. Having more than one credit card probably means paying more than one annual fee. If you have six major credit cards at an average annual fee of $35, that's $175 you could save every year by closing five of the accounts. If your annual fees are higher, you'll save even more by consolidating.

257. Look at the big picture when choosing and using credit cards. Rebate credit cards (frequent flyer miles, cash back, etc.) only benefit you if you don't carry a balance. If you do, interest costs will more than erase any gains you receive in rebates.

258. Don't pay for tuition, room and board, or textbooks with credit cards unless you're sure you're going to be able to pay the balance off very soon. Otherwise you'd be better off in the long run to take out a student loan, for two reasons: one, the interest rate is much lower on student loans; and two, you can deduct some of the interest expense on student loans. Interest on credit card debt is never deductible for income tax purposes.

259. Use one of the many online tools to help you decide which credit card is the best deal: a higher interest rate card with no annual fee or a lower rate card with an annual fee. One such calculator can be found at www.finance-center.com/cards.htm.

260. If you carry a balance on your credit card, you can save money by paying the bill the day it arrives rather than waiting until the due date. When you carry a balance, interest is calculated from the first day of the purchase; there is no grace period. The longer you wait to make your payment, the more interest will accrue.

261. Make a point of looking at the finance charge on your credit card statements every month. This reality check may make you pause the next time you're tempted to pay with plastic.

262. Call your credit card company and ask them to lower your interest rate. If you have a good payment history, your request will often be granted. Talk about easy ways to save money!

263. Lenders aren't the only ones leery of people who have lots of available credit but limited income, like most college students. Landlords and businesses don't want to be left holding the bag if you run up credit card debt you have no way to repay, so these businesses may charge you higher prices or require higher deposits in order to protect themselves. You can avoid this by having lower credit limits.

264. Getting into credit card debt in college may increase the time it takes to get your degree and how much your education costs in the long run. Studies have found that students with credit card debt are often forced to reduce their class load so they can work more to make their monthly credit card payments.

265. When you use a credit card, the merchant has to pay a fee of 2 to 4 percent to the credit card company, which reduces his profit. Pay cash and ask for a cash discount on large items. You may or may not get one, but it doesn't hurt to ask.

Protect Yourself from Credit Card Fraud and Identity Theft

266. Credit card fraud is common in dorms because so many people live in one building in an unusually open environment. Keep close tabs on your credit card and don't leave it lying around or leave your wallet or purse lying around if the card is in it. All anyone needs to commit fraud is the number and expiration date from your card. It's best to keep it locked up until you need it.

267. Thieves who "dumpster dive" can retrieve credit card offers, apply for credit in your name, and charge up a huge balance before you even know what happened. They can also use personal information they find on statements and other documents containing personal information. An inexpensive shredder should be required equipment in every college dorm room. Shred credit card offers you receive in the mail and any documents containing personal information before you throw them in the trash.

268. Save your credit card slips each time you make a purchase and keep them together until your monthly statement arrives. As soon as you receive it, check each slip against the statement and verify that the amount is accurate. If you find a discrepancy, call the credit card issuer immediately. One common scam that has netted its perpetrators big bucks is charging small amounts to many credit cards, hoping the credit card owner will ignore it.

269. Write down your credit card numbers, expiration dates, and the names, addresses, and phone numbers of the issuing companies, and keep the information in a secure place. If your card is lost or stolen, notify the card issuer immediately to take advantage of the law that limits your liability for fraudulent use of your card.

270. If you have an issue with a charge that appears on your credit card statement, notify the credit card company in writing within 60 days (preferably much sooner) by sending a letter to the address specified on your statement (not the payment address). Your lender is required to respond within 30 days and conduct an investigation within 90 days. Until the issue is resolved, you're not required to pay the amount in question.

271. Some universities let you choose your student identification number. Never use your Social Security Number as your student ID number if you have a choice. Having your Social Security Number prominently displayed on a card that you use so frequently makes you a prime target for identity theft.

272. Credit cards are not to be shared, even with your best friend. Guard your credit card number and give it out only when ordering online or over the phone. Order in private so your number won't be overheard.

273. If possible, keep your credit card in sight while it's being scanned for purchases. Fraud committed by salespeople and restaurant wait staff who skim the information from your card with a special hand-held scanner is on the increase. The scammers sell the information to others who use it to commit fraud with your credit card number.

274. Check your credit reports once a year. You can correct any errors that might end up raising your interest rates, and ensure that you haven't been a victim of identity theft. If you see any credit accounts on your report that you don't recognize, contact the credit bureau immediately. Someone else might be fraudulently applying for and using credit in your name.

275. College students are prime targets for identity theft, so if you live in a dorm or other shared living area, take precautions to protect your personal and credit information. Keep financial and personal information in a safe place out of view from prying eyes. Protect your wallet, checkbook, credit card receipts, and incoming and outgoing mail. Keep your dorm room locked when you're not in it.

276. Use a free computer firewall program like Zone Alarm (www.zonelabs.com) to protect yourself from hackers who can retrieve financial or other information you have stored on your computer. This information can be used to apply for credit in your name or steal money from your accounts.

277. Never download a computer file that is sent from someone you don't know. Such files often contain viruses or Trojan horses that install code on your computer. Your personal information can then be stolen and used fraudulently.

278. Reduce your chances of being a victim of identity theft by keeping tight control of your personal financial information. Shred bills, statements, credit card offers, and credit card receipts before trashing them.

279. To protect yourself from identity theft, don't provide personal information such as address, telephone number, Social Security Number, bank account number, or email address unless you know to whom you're providing the information, why it's being requested, and how it will be used. Don't give out personal information over the phone unless you initiated the call and you know the organization.

280. Beware of phishing emails, which appear to be sent from AOL, eBay, your bank or credit card company, PayPal, or other seemingly legitimate businesses, warning you that your account information needs to be updated. The message urges you to click on the link embedded in the email, which takes you to an official looking website where you enter your credit card or bank account information. Thieves use this information to steal you blind. Never respond to emails asking for this type of information.

Four Sources of Help with Credit Card Debt When You're in over Your Head

281. If you start to encounter financial problems, seek help immediately from your parents or a financial counselor or credit counselor. Getting a grip on your finances early will make life easier in the long run. The longer you wait to take action, the worse your situation could get and the more painful it will be to extricate yourself.

282. If you're having trouble paying your credit card or other bills, free counseling may be available from your credit union, cooperative extension office, military family service center, or religious organization. Don't wait. Call at the first sign of trouble.

283. You can also obtain free professional counseling services from a member of the National Foundation for Consumer Credit, which operates under the name Consumer Credit Counseling Service (CCCS). To locate a CCCS near you, call toll-free 1-800-388-2227 or visit www.nfcc.org.

284. Myvesta is another counseling service (Internet based) that can help you get control of your debt before it's too late. If you're feeling like you're in over your head, visit their website at www.myvesta.org for more information.

Two Sources of Credit "Help" You Should Avoid

285. Don't believe services that claim they can erase your bad credit. They'll take your money and leave you in the same shape in which they found you. Bad credit can only be "fixed" by using credit responsibly and making your payments consistently over a period of months or years; however, if there's an actual error on your credit report, you should try to clear it up by sending a letter of 100 words or less to the credit bureau, explaining the problem.

286. If, in spite of your good intentions, you find yourself in deep credit card debt, stay away from so-called credit doctors or anyone who promises to fix your bad credit for free or for a fee that ranges between $300 and $1,000. These offers are one of the biggest scams that desperate people fall for when they're over their heads in debt.

Protect Your Credit Score

287. Understand the consequences of bad credit. If you have a low credit score, you won't be able to open a checking account, get another credit card, sign a lease, buy furniture or a car or anything else on credit, or get a mortgage. You'll pay higher insurance premiums. Employers may deny you a job.

288. After you've had your first credit card for six months or a year, obtain a copy of your credit report from each of the major reporting bureaus: Experian (1-800-311-4769), TransUnion (1-800-888-4213), and Equifax (1-800-685-1111). Creditors don't always report to all three major credit bureaus, so to get an accurate picture of your standing, it's important to get a copy of all three reports. Review them carefully and correct any errors.

289. Negative information stays on your credit report for seven years, so if you damage your credit history now, not only will you pay higher interest rates almost immediately, the bad news will follow you well past your college years. Know what affects your credit rating; for example, too many credit cards (even if they have a zero balance), using too much of your available line of credit, and applying for multiple cards in a short time period.

290. If you pay your Macy's bill late, the interest rate may go up not only on your Macy's account, but also on your other major credit cards. Other creditors see your slip-up on your credit report and figure they're at risk, even though you've paid them on time so far. Some creditors even review your credit report occasionally hoping to find such black marks as an excuse to charge you a higher rate.

291. If you mess up your credit score by having negative credit information on your credit report, your interest rates could jump to as much as 28 percent because you'll be considered a bad risk. Guard your credit score religiously.

292. If you receive an actual credit card that you didn't apply for in the mail, cut it up into small pieces and mail it back to the credit card company asking them to close the account. Send a letter to the credit reporting bureaus notifying them that you didn't request the card and have returned it to the sender. Otherwise, it will show up on your credit report and affect your ability to be approved for loans.

293. Don't think you can take care of burdensome credit card debt by declaring bankruptcy, which stays on your credit report for seven to ten years. During that time, you'll be hard pressed to get any kind of credit like a car loan, mortgage, or installment loan, and you'll have trouble renting an apartment, getting utilities in your name, and maybe even finding a job.

294. Large unused credit limits can lower your credit score and make you less attractive to lenders because you could charge up to the limit at any time. Don't let your credit card company boost your credit limit beyond what you can comfortably afford to repay. Take control by calling the company and asking them to reduce your limit.

295. Don't apply for multiple credit cards just to get the freebies. Having numerous credit cards hurts your credit record, even if you never charge anything to them. Lenders look at your combined credit limits as debt waiting to happen.

296. Every time you apply for credit, a notation is made in your credit report. Lenders frown on multiple credit applications because people with multiple credit cards are considered a higher risk. Lenders may deny you credit or slap you with a higher interest rate when they see multiple credit applications in your credit history file. If you're shopping for a card with better terms, submit your applications within a thirty-day timeframe to avoid a black mark in your credit history.

6.

Manage Your Student Loans

There are three cardinal rules to follow with student loans: 1) borrow only what you need, 2) manage your money wisely, and 3) keep track of what you owe. Managing your student loans includes managing all of your money, because if you overspend, you'll have to overborrow. Every dollar wasted or spent carelessly is a dollar you'll borrow later and another dollar plus interest you'll have to repay.

297. Use student loans to finance your education, not your lifestyle. You'll be paying them off for a long time, so spend the money on things that are directly related to your education, like tuition, room and board, and books. It doesn't make sense to use this money for basic living expenses like clothes, groceries, and entertainment.

298. Remember that the amount you'll have to repay on your student loans will be significantly more than the amount you borrowed because of the interest expense you'll incur. When you think of the amount you've borrowed in student loans, add at least 30 percent to it so you have a realistic number in your head of what you'll really owe.

299. For most people, a college education requires sacrifice. You can sacrifice now or you can sacrifice during the years you're repaying your loans. Don't bury your head in the sand when it comes to managing your student loans. Know the exact total and the amount your payments will be, based on what you've borrowed so far, and do your best to minimize the amount you have to borrow.

300. Don't take your parents' ability to contribute financially to your college education for granted. Most parents of college students channel money to their kids at the expense of funding their retirement. You have many years to pay off student loan debt, but your parents have a very limited time to build their retirement nest egg, so don't make their sacrifices greater than necessary. Spending your money wisely will benefit both you and your parents.

301. When calculating how much student loan money you need, ask yourself these questions: Can you reduce your expenses? Work more during the school year without jeopardizing your grades? Work more during the summer or find a higher paying job? Have you done your homework on searching for scholarship money? The more money you can earn and the more you can reduce spending, the less you'll have to borrow (and repay).

302. Don't assume that you'll get the best deal from a "preferred lender" listed on your college's website. Listing preferred lenders is yet another way that some colleges are making money off students by accepting a kickback or some type of financial consideration when students sign up for loans. These "preferred lender" loans can cost you considerably more than other loans, so be sure to shop around to find the best deal.

Eight Warnings about Student Loans

303. Before you take out student loans, think long and hard about how committed you are to finishing your degree. Whether you graduate or not, you'll have to pay off your student loans. It's difficult enough when you have a degree and a good job, so imagine having to pay off tens of thousands of dollars when you have no degree and no marketable skills that qualify you for a higher-paying job.

304. Even bankruptcy will not release you from your student loan commitment, so never take a student loan for more than you absolutely need, and never use it on anything but college essentials. You're obligated to repay student loans even if you never graduate or you can't find a job after graduation.

305. No matter what kind of financial tangle you get yourself into while in college, you'll never escape your unpaid student loans because they can never be wiped out except by participating in a loan forgiveness program offered for graduates in certain fields. Think twice about spending that student loan money on parties, clothes, and spring breaks.

306. When you take out a student loan, you're making a commitment that lasts longer than most marriages, so make borrowing your last resort. First, exhaust all the possibilities for grants, scholarships, work-study programs, and other options available to you. Use every trick in the book to control your living expenses and other college costs to avoid graduating with tens of thousands of dollars of student loan debt that will take between ten and twenty years to repay.

307. Before you take out a loan for your education, think about the obligation you're taking on and your ability to repay your student loans. If you don't repay the loan according to the terms of the promissory note you signed, you'll be considered in default, which has serious consequences, including a negative impact on your credit score.

308. Don't fall into the trap of borrowing money for college based on what you think you'll be able to earn after graduation. If you fail to consider the fact that your starting salary may be lower than you anticipate and it will probably take you several years to build up to your expected salary, you may have a tough few years after graduation as you struggle to make your student loan payments. Underestimate the salary you expect to earn for the first few years of your career when calculating the amount of money you can comfortably afford to repay after graduation.

309. If you have to cut back on your classes in order to earn more money for college, beware of dropping below half-time status (usually viewed as six credit hours per semester). To continue to be eligible for deferment of your student loans, you must qualify as at least a half-time student. Otherwise, your student loans become due within six months, even though you're still in school.

310. If you're having trouble making your student loan payments, get help immediately. Defaulting on your student loans will damage your credit far into the future and will preclude you from obtaining any additional financial aid.

311. Don't borrow against the future to support an unrealistic lifestyle while you are in college. Before student loans were so prevalent, college students were frugal by necessity and they graduated with much lower debt. Skimp and go without now and you'll be far ahead financially when you graduate.

312. The longer you take to pay off your student loans, the more they'll end up costing you. Pick a payment schedule that's realistic but will allow you to repay your loans as quickly as possible.

313. If you have a choice between a subsidized student loan and an unsubsidized student loan, choose the subsidized student loan first. The government or your school will pay the interest on subsidized loans while you're in college. You're responsible for the interest on unsubsidized loans, and can either postpone the interest payments until graduation or pay the interest while you're in school. Postponing payments will cost you more in the long run.

314. It's easy to have a false sense of security about your ability to pay off your student loan debt because payments can be deferred until after you graduate. If you work during the semester, consider beginning repayment while you're still in school. You'll be less likely to borrow more than you need and you'll be more likely to manage your student loan money carefully. You'll also reduce your interest costs.

315. Don't take out a bigger student loan than you absolutely must have to get through the semester. It's much too tempting to spend it on nonessentials. You can always apply for additional loans later if you need the money for the next semester or school year.

316. If you have student loan money left over after paying your tuition, room and board, and books for the semester, either give it back to the lender or put it in a separate bank account. You'll be less likely to fritter it away on nonessentials if it's not in your checking account.

317. The interest rates on savings accounts may be so low they hardly seem worth bothering with, but even a little bit of interest will help offset the interest you're incurring on the borrowed money. Place all but your monthly living money in a savings or money market account so it will earn a little interest.

318. If you plan to be a childcare provider, nurse, doctor, nurse practitioner, physician's assistant, midwife, dentist, dental hygienist, psychologist, lawyer, or teacher, you may be eligible to have part of your Stafford loan wiped off the slate by working for two years in a low-income area after graduation. Check with your student loan provider for details.

319. If you complete a two-year term in the Peace Corps, you can wipe out 30 percent of your Perkins loan balance. You may also be able to defer your student loan payments while serving in the Peace Corps.

320. If you have to take out student loans, try to take them in this order to save money: Federal Perkins loans, Federal Subsidized Stafford or Direct loans, Federal Unsubsidized Stafford or Direct loans, and Alternative loans.

321. How much is too much? Lenders consider monthly student loan payments exceeding 8 percent of your monthly income to be unmanageable. If you make $40,000 a year after graduation, student loan payments of $266 per month will put you into this category. Most graduates begin their career in lower paying entry-level jobs and it takes several years to earn the salary they expect, so the debt burden may be greater than they think.

322. A study by the Cambridge Consumer Credit Index indicated that 75 percent of college graduates with outstanding student loans say the loan payments prevent them from making major purchases such as a house or car. The higher your student loans, the less disposable income you'll have left over for everyday spending and major purchases, so use your student loan money wisely. Borrow only for essentials so you can enjoy the income from your job after graduation.

323. Be smart about borrowing. Base your student loans on your best estimate of how much money you'll need for necessities, not on how much the lender will lend you. Use an online student loan payment calculator to calculate what your payments will be.

324. When dealing with large amounts of money from student loans or scholarships at one time it's easy to misjudge how far that money will actually go. Write down the sum on a piece of paper and deduct all the expenses that the money needs to cover, like books, groceries, tuition, transportation, and entertainment. Divide the remainder by the number of weeks left before you get your next large payment; that's how much you can spend on everything else each week. Having this perspective will help you avoid overspending and running out of money.

325. Just because the financial aid award letter says you're eligible for a certain loan amount doesn't mean you have to borrow the whole amount. By reducing your expenses, sticking to a spending plan, and working part-time, you can reduce the amount you need to borrow, making life after college much more enjoyable when it comes time to pay off the loans.

326. If money is tight or you have to borrow a large amount to attend a private college, consider a state university instead. Tuition and fees at private schools average four times higher than public schools.

327. It's easy to borrow more than you can afford to pay because needs-based student loans don't require any payments while you're still in school. Calculate how much you need for necessities for the school year and borrow only that much. You can always borrow more later if you really need it.

328. If possible, pay the interest on your unsubsidized loans while you're in college. You can defer the interest until graduation, but you'll end up paying more because the interest compounds while you're not making payments.

329. Lower monthly payments on your student loans results in a longer repayment period, which means more interest expense. Keep this in mind when choosing repayment periods.

330. Seek immediate assistance if you feel unable to make a loan payment on time. The consequences of defaulting include being denied credit cards, mortgages, and car loans; incurring legal fees; having your wages garnished to repay the loan; having all your student loans immediately become payable in full; being denied other types of federal financial assistance; having your income tax refunds seized; being harassed by collectors, and other unpleasant actions.

331. Many student loan lenders offer discounts and incentives if you have your student loan payments automatically deducted from your checking or savings account each month and you make timely payments for a period of consecutive months. Take advantage of this easy way to reduce your interest rate and the total cost of your student loans.

332. If you've started repayment of your student loans, make sure you make the full payment on time every month even if you've lost your coupon book or you never received one. Otherwise you'll be considered in default. Partial payments are not acceptable and will also place you in default.

333. Find out the details of any student loans you're offered, such as repayment terms and interest rates. Compare the loans so you can make intelligent decisions about which ones to accept based on all the facts. This will help you minimize your borrowing costs.

334. Keep track of the student aid you've received so far by visiting the U.S. Department of Education's National Student Loan Data System (NSLDS) website at www.studentaid.ed.gov. This central database coordinates information sent from the various financial aid providers into one place that's accessible to students. You can view your loan and grant amounts, the status of your loans, outstanding balances, and disbursements. Keeping tabs on this information can also help ensure you don't miss a payment.

7.

Save Money When Paying for Your Education

Getting an education involves hundreds of decisions that affect your wallet, now and for years to come. Your biggest expenses will be tuition, room and board, books, and fees, so these areas yield the largest savings potential. Nowhere is it more important to see the big picture.

335. Deciding which college to attend has social, emotional, and financial repercussions. Before making your decision, make sure the school offers the program and courses you want and the services and activities you're interested in. Find out what crimes occur on campus, what financial aid is available, and the refund policy if you enroll but don't attend classes. Transferring to another school can be expensive, so doing this homework up front can save you a lot of money.

336. Look beyond the cost of tuition when evaluating the cost of attending various colleges. Tuition is one of the biggest college expenses, but room and board, transportation, and fees are also a significant portion of your educational costs and can vary widely between schools. If your main comparison when evaluating the cost of each school is tuition, your college education could end up costing you a lot more than you bargained for. Look at the big picture to make the best decision.

337. It's interesting to know that the leaders of most of the top corporations in America and the governors of most states graduated from colleges that many of us have never heard of. Getting a degree from an expensive school doesn't guarantee that you'll earn more money or be more successful, so keep that in mind when choosing a school.

338. Rather than going deeply into debt in order to get a college degree, consider working full-time and attending college in the evenings. More schools are catering to working students and increasing their offerings of night courses. You can take a three-credit course by attending class one night a week for two to three hours, saving you time and commuting costs and allowing you to continue earning a salary while you attend school.

339. If you're not sure what you want to major in, it's okay to take a year or two to decide while you get your general education requirements out of the way. After that, the more you delay, the more your education is likely to cost because you may not be able to fit in all your required classes in time to graduate in four years.

340. If you're concerned about having enough money to get through four years of college, consider starting out at a community college and transferring to a university after two years. You can get most of your general education requirements out of the way at a much lower cost, yet still earn your degree from the college of your choice. The total cost of your education will be dramatically lower than if you had spent all four years at a four-year school.

341. Tuition and room and board are not the only costs you should consider when choosing a college. You'll pay more for everything—food, clothing, gas, entertainment, and transportation—in some college towns just because the cost of living is higher in that area. The difference can be substantial, so check out the cost of living in the areas you're considering for college.

342. If cash is tight and you can't pay your entire tuition bill in a lump sum at the beginning of the semester, ask your college about deferred payment plans or monthly tuition payment plans. Spreading the payments out may prevent you from having to borrow and pay interest expenses. You'll have to manage your money carefully to make sure you'll have the cash when the tuition bill comes due, but it will give you time to earn more money.

343. You'll be tempted to take electives based on your personal interests, and that's good, to a point. Plan ahead and make sure you'll be able to fit in all your general ed classes and the courses required for your major so you can finish your degree in four years. Once a year, sit down with a counselor in your school's career center to make sure you're on track. An extra semester or two can cost you over $10,000.

344. At many schools, taking the minimum number of credits to qualify as a full-time student may not be enough to allow you to graduate in four years. The longer it takes to get your degree, the more it will cost. Even one extra semester adds thousands of dollars to your education bill, so plan ahead.

Cut Your Costs by Accelerating Your Degree

345. Why spend your time and money on those boring freshman-level courses when you can dive right into the interesting stuff? While you're still in high school, test out of basic courses on subjects you're already knowledgeable about, such as math, science, social studies, accounting, or psychology. The test fees for programs like the College Level Examination Program (CLEP), Dantes Subject Standardized Tests (DSST), Excelsior College Exams (ECE), and Advanced Placement (AP) are cheaper than tuition, plus you'll reduce the amount of time it'll take you to finish your degree.

346. If you've taken Advanced Placement (AP), College Level Examination Program (CLEP) tests, or other exams for credit, make sure they show up on your transcript right away so you don't waste time taking unnecessary classes. In college, time is definitely money.

347. If you're planning to get a bachelor's and a master's degree, check out some of the hundreds of schools that offer accelerated degrees: a combined bachelor's and master's degree program in five years. You can often shave a year off your total college time by taking advantage of these programs, while saving thousands of dollars in tuition, room and board, and the cost of applying to grad schools.

348. Some schools offer accelerated classes that cram a semester's worth of material into a six- or eight-week session. If you can handle the increased intensity, you can shave a year and 25 percent to 50 percent of your college expenses off your education bill.

349. Get academic credit for off-campus work. Talk to your advisor, professor, or department head about receiving credit for work that's related to your major. You'll earn spending money and get course credits at the same time.

350. Take a class or two during the summer at a less expensive college, like a community college near your home. You can get some of your general education requirements out of the way with the goal of shaving a semester off your degree program, which will save you thousands of dollars. Be sure to check with your college first to make sure the credits will transfer.

351. Drastically cut your education expenses by taking advantage of distance learning. You can earn an associate's, bachelor's, or master's degree online while keeping your day job. Research your options on Peterson's Distance Learning site at www.petersons.com/distancelearning.asp. The site offers additional information and tools such as the distance learning assessment, which helps you determine if distance learning is right for you.

352. Accelerate your four-year degree and graduate in three years simply by taking classes in the summer. You could work part-time while attending classes if you're willing to work hard. Besides being able to begin your career (and earn the big bucks) a year sooner, you'll cut a significant amount off the cost of your education.

353. If you're returning to college after a long absence, be sure to get the maximum amount of credit for your former classes. The admissions office will evaluate your transcript and tell you how many credits have been approved for transfer, but don't settle for this number. Study the school's course catalog to find a class that corresponds to each class you previously took that was not accepted for transfer, then challenge the decision by writing an explanation of why you feel the class requirement should be waived. This may take some work and you may have to go to the top of the admissions department for approval, but you could save a lot of time and money.

354. It may be possible to get in-state tuition rates at an out-of-state school under certain circumstances. For instance, if your state university doesn't offer a major in your chosen field of study and your state has a reciprocal agreement with another state, you'll be able to attend the out-of-state school but pay in-state rates.

355. Some states have fairly liberal rules about establishing residency, allowing you to pay in-state tuition rates at an out-of-state school. Low population states in the Midwest sometimes offer this incentive. Check with the school to find out what the state residency requirements are in that state.

356. Consider going to the state university in your home state, where a college education is likely to cost less than half that of a private school. Many state schools have excellent programs in a variety of fields of study. For most careers, the degree itself is more important than where you got it.

357. Enjoy the benefit of in-state tuition rates at the public school of your choice by moving to that state before you enroll in school and working for six months or a year to establish residency. This could delay the start of your education, but if you need to work to earn some money first anyway, you can kill two birds with one stone.

358. Tuition and room and board should be your biggest priorities, with everything else being secondary. Manage your money carefully so you can make all tuition payments on time and avoid the hefty late fee imposed by your college.

359. Some colleges have begun offering tuition discounts on classes taken at unpopular times, such as before 9:00 a.m. or after 3:00 p.m. Find out if your school offers this type of discount, and if it does, adapt your schedule to fit in a few courses at the discounted rate. Over the course of a four-year degree, your savings could be significant.

360. Take as many credits each semester as you can reasonably handle and you'll get more value for your tuition dollars. Taking less than a full load raises your cost per credit hour and can result in significantly higher tuition costs overall. By taking a full load, you may be able to finish in three-and-a-half years and save thousands of dollars.

361. If you participate in the Reserve Officers Training Corps (ROTC) during high school, you could receive scholarships that cover full tuition, books, and fees and provide a monthly living allowance. All branches of the U.S. Armed Forces offer this federal merit-based scholarship program.

362. Every little bit helps when it comes to paying for college. If you're working while attending classes, find out if your employer offers a tuition assistance plan. Under these plans, eligible employees are reimbursed for part of their tuition costs if they achieve an acceptable grade in the class. For qualified plans, the reimbursement, up to a certain dollar amount, is not considered taxable income to you.

363. Your employer may be willing to foot the bill for job-related courses at the local university or community college even if they don't offer a formal tuition assistance plan. Improving your skills makes you a more valuable employee. Write a proposal demonstrating how the course of study you want to pursue will improve your job skills and present it to your employer.

364. If you have the cash available or you have student loan money sitting in a bank account, consider taking advantage of your school's tuition prepayment discounts. You could save hundreds of dollars. This is a good use of extra student loan money because it eliminates the temptation to fritter away the money on nonessentials. The discounts are likely to be greater than any interest you'd earn by leaving the money in a savings account until the next tuition payment is due.

365. Find out if your college offers a tuition lock-in for the four years you'll be attending. Some schools will lock-in your tuition rate for the entire four years you're in college; others will do so for a fee. With the rate of tuition increases escalating, this option is worth consideration.

366. If you work on campus, you may be able to receive a tuition waiver in addition to your hourly pay, which could save you hundreds or even thousands of dollars. Ask your student employment office about which jobs include tuition waivers.

Be Creative When Buying Textbooks

367. When you're ready to sell your textbooks back to the bookstore, don't expect to get even close to what you paid for them. If your book is in demand, you'll be lucky if you get 20 percent of the original price, even if you never opened the book and it's in pristine condition. If there's a new edition of the book or there's not much demand for it, you may get only 10 percent of the original price, or the bookstore may refuse to buy it back at all. Look for alternative places to sell textbooks when you're finished with them.

368. One easy way to find the best deals on textbooks is the textbook search engine www.bestbookbuys.com, which compares prices at twenty-five online bookstores and reports the cost, including shipping and tax, for both new and used books from various stores. Be sure to consider the cost of shipping when comparing prices.

369. Many expenses are bunched into the first few weeks of the semester. If you find yourself short of cash, buy your books as you need them instead of all at once. You may even find you don't need some of the books at all.

370. Don't be overzealous when buying textbooks. Professors often require certain books and recommend others. Skip the recommended ones; you may never need them. If you do, the professor may have reserved them at the library or you could borrow them from someone in your class or dorm.

371. Buy used textbooks. So what if the book's former owner has run amok with a highlighter? The cost of used textbooks is roughly half that of new textbooks, which average over $100 each. With the total cost of books per student averaging close to $1,000 per year, the savings of buying used books can add up quickly, and those highlighted areas may even make your studying easier.

372. If you're looking for used textbooks, the earlier you get to the bookstore, the better luck you'll have getting the books you need. Used books sell very fast because everybody loves a bargain, and there's usually not enough supply to cover the demand for popular classes.

373. Work in the campus bookstore and earn a discount on books and supplies. With the average price of a new textbook weighing in at a hefty $100, a 25 percent discount could save you a bundle over the course of the year.

374. Don't assume you need to buy a new textbook just because there's a new edition. Often, new editions have very few substantial changes; they're a method used by publishers to increase their sales. A used copy of last semester's edition will often be adequate. If you're unsure, ask your instructor.

375. Sell your used textbooks as soon after the end of the semester as possible. The better condition they're in, the better price you'll get for them, so if possible, don't write in them, highlight them, allow them to get wet, or get food on them.

376. Instead of selling your used textbooks back to the college bookstore at a small percentage of what you paid for them, sell them directly to other students by announcing their availability using campus wide email or sell them to friends and dormmates who are taking the class next semester. Bookstores typically resell used books at around 75 percent of the original cost, so if you charged between 50 and 75 percent, both you and the buyer would come out ahead.

377. Check out a few of the textbook websites like:
- www.cheapesttextbooks.com
- www.ecampus.com
- www.efollet.com
- www.varsitybooks.com
- www.amazon.com
- www.barnesandnoble.com

378. eBay is another good place to buy used textbooks, but before buying at online auction sites, familiarize yourself with the average going price of the books you're interested in so you don't overpay by getting caught up in the bidding process.

379. If you order textbooks online, do so as much in advance as possible so you don't have to pay for overnight shipping, which can cost three or more times as much as UPS ground or U.S. Postal Service media mail. This could wipe out any savings.

380. At the beginning of the semester, go to the book buyback location in your college bookstore and talk to other students standing in line waiting to sell their books. If you find someone who's planning to sell a book you need, make an offer that will benefit you both. You'll get the book for significantly less than the bookstore price (even for used books) and the seller will get more than the bookstore will likely offer them.

381. Ask friends if they know anyone who has taken the courses you're planning to take. Students often hang onto books in their major or may not have had a chance to try to sell books back yet. They may let you borrow books or rent them for a reasonable fee.

382. Some college towns have independent bookstores that sell new and used textbooks. Their prices may be cheaper than the prices in the campus bookstore. Look in the telephone book Yellow Pages or online for nearby bookstores.

383. Save receipts for all textbooks you purchase. If you have to drop a class, or you find a book is not required after all, you can get a refund as long as the book still looks like new and you haven't written in it or highlighted anything.

384. Before you buy new or used textbooks, check with friends or fellow dorm dwellers to see if one of them has textbooks you could borrow for any of your classes. Being able to avoid buying even one new book a semester can save you several hundred dollars per year.

385. Hang out in the hallway where a class you plan to take next semester is having final exams and ask exiting students if they'd like to sell their textbook. They may even be willing to sell for the same price the bookstore would pay them, just to avoid the hassle of spending a morning in the book buyback line. Don't forget to have some cash in your pocket.

386. On the class syllabus, many instructors list required or suggested supplemental books in addition to the main textbook. Delay buying the supplemental books until you're sure the instructor will use them. Often only short sections of these books are ever assigned for reading, and you can easily borrow the book from the library or a fellow student.

387. If you're an entrepreneurial type and you have a place to store a few books, you could have your own business as an online book reseller. Choose an online used book vendor, set up an account, and list the books you have available and their condition (be honest). If you sell directly to buyers, the online bookseller will take a percentage, usually around 15 percent; if you sell directly to the online bookseller and they have to find a buyer, they'll take more of a cut. Either way, you could make a handy little profit by buying books from other students and selling them online.

388. It's tempting to hang on to books that are related to your major, but think twice before doing this. By the time you graduate from college, the books might be outdated and useless, especially science or technology-related books. Sell the books back, pocket the cash, and if you need reference books when you start working in your field, you can always buy them then.

Save Money by Avoiding Fees on Campus

389. Don't use a shotgun approach to applying to colleges, firing off an application to every school that sparks your interest. Those applications usually require a fee, so before shelling out all that money, do some research in your guidance office, public library, or online. Narrow your choices down to just a few schools that you're really interested in.

390. Decide on your classes as soon as possible and register early. If you register late, you'll incur a service fee and you may not get the class you want.

391. Before registering for classes, find out all you can about each class to be sure it's one you need and want, the class time will fit your schedule, and your total course load will be manageable. If you change your mind after registration, you'll incur add/drop charges.

392. Some students change majors several times before settling on one. Be aware that every time you change your major, you may incur a fee. Try to wait until you're reasonably sure before you officially change majors.

393. To avoid paying late fees, pay all your bills on time and return all borrowed items when due (library books, rental videos). For many students, various types of late fees add up to significant sums. Paying late fees is like throwing money away, and is usually a result of poor planning and overspending.

394. Pay bills online, especially credit card bills, to avoid late fees. If you miss your payment date by even one day, you'll incur a hefty late fee and get dinged on your credit score. With online banking, you can plan ahead and not have to worry about the U.S. Postal Service delivering your payment late or your check sitting in a log-jam in the mailroom.

395. It's expensive to drive a car on campus, so whenever possible, leave your wheels at home. Parking permits can cost several hundred dollars per semester, and buying one doesn't guarantee you'll find a parking space when you need it.

396. Keep close tabs on your student ID card and your meal card. If you lose or misplace one of them, you'll be charged $15 to $20 for a replacement.

397. If you make an appointment at the student health center and change your mind or for some reason can't keep your appointment, be sure to call ahead to let them know. Otherwise, you could be charged a no-show fee.

398. Make sure you have the money set aside for your next tuition payment well before the due date. Missing the tuition payment date will cost you between $50 and $100 in fees. If you make your payment on time but your check bounces, your school could charge you as much as $60 on top of the fees your bank will charge for insufficient funds.

399. If you cause damage to your dorm room or the common areas, you'll be assessed a fee when you move out. Even a little thing like leaving tape on the walls could result in a fee. Before you move out, check the space carefully and fix anything that needs fixing.

8.

Mind over Money

You're on your own for the first time, and having complete control over your own money is a heady feeling. There's nobody to answer to on a day-to-day basis, you've just received what seems like a lot of cash in the form of financial aid, and you're feeling flush. You may get a temporary psychological high when you spend money, especially when you buy on credit, but spending uncontrollably can put you on a roller coaster of brief euphoric highs and long, depressing lows. Controlling your spending is a challenge, but will prevent stress later. Think of it as a game that you play against yourself. You'll always come out the winner.

400. College students sometimes feel pressured to buy expensive clothing or other items to look good to other students, but you can't buy approval or friendship. College is a time for learning how to manage your money and getting by on as little as possible as you spend huge amounts on your education to qualify yourself for a well-paying career. Don't get caught up in buying things because you believe they'll make others think more highly of you.

401. Don't use money as a substitute for emotional needs, like love, power, acceptance, or social status. In the long run, it doesn't work. It may feel good for a moment, but the feeling is fleeting.

402. Identify what triggers your spending. This takes a little introspection, self-awareness, and a willingness to be honest with yourself. Awareness is your first line of defense against overspending.

403. To find out if you're a compulsive spender, ask yourself these questions (be honest, now): Do I have a feel-good moment when I buy something? Do I compare my stuff to other people's stuff? Do I feel that people who have more material things than I do are better than me? If you answered yes to one or more of these questions, you're using money for psychological reasons and should seek help before your spending gets out of control.

404. Spending money to change your mood is a very temporary fix and becomes addictive. The consequences could be a lifetime struggle with unmanageable debt. When you get the urge to shop, stop and analyze how you're feeling and what stress or other emotions may be contributing to your impulse to spend. Acknowledging those feelings is sometimes all it takes to control the urge to splurge.

405. If you consistently spend beyond your means, you may have a deep emotional problem. The sooner you admit it and seek help, the less debt you'll have to pay off. Find a consumer credit counseling center near you or ask your financial aid office for a recommendation. If you still can't control your spending, you may also want to seek psychological counseling to get to the bottom of the issues that make you use money in an unhealthy manner.

406. Don't use things to bolster your confidence or self-esteem. These feelings can't be bought, and trying to obtain them by spending money leads to distorted values, financial difficulties, and emotional problems. Improve your confidence and self-esteem by doing things that make you feel good about yourself.

407. You can do things you want with your money while you're in college, but you can't do everything you want. Life is all about choices, so decide which things matter most to you and which things you can live without for now.

Five Ways to Become Financially Literate

408. Today's financial world is very complex, and you won't learn everything you need to know in order to be financially successful unless you make an effort to educate yourself. Take a personal finance class at your college or from a local organization, and then practice what you've learned. It's better to learn through classroom education than through the school of hard knocks, and you'll feel good about being in control of your money and your life.

409. When you're tempted to spend money on want rather than need, remember the message in the bestseller *The Millionaire Next Door*: Wealth is accumulated, not spent. It's usually the result of a lifestyle of hard work, planning, and self-discipline with money.

410. Find out if there's a chapter of Students in Free Enterprise (SIFE) operating at your college. SIFE partners with businesses and colleges to teach students about free enterprise. At some colleges, SIFE offers workshops that teach money management skills to college students. To find out if they're available in your community, visit www.sife.org.

411. Read a good book about basic personal finance, such as *Everything Personal Finance in Your 20s and 30s* by Debby Fowles or *The Complete Idiot's Guide to Personal Finance in Your 20s and 30s* by Sarah Young Fisher. Consider it one of the most important textbooks you will ever buy.

412. Adopt a spending plan early in your first semester so you can keep track of how much money you'll need, how much you've got, and whether you're staying on track or falling behind. Use a budget spreadsheet like the one at financialplan.about.com/library/blcollbudget.htm. You'll have the peace of mind of knowing you have enough money to get through the school year, or plenty of advance warning that you're going to fall short.

413. Budgets have a negative connotation for some people, but think of them as a way to ensure you won't run out of money before you run out of months. A budget is a tool that will help you manage your money and keep your spending under control.

414. To create a budget, list your sources of income, such as savings from your summer jobs, financial support from your parents, financial aid, scholarships, and job income. Then list your expenses, such as tuition, books, fees, groceries, gas, and entertainment in as much detail as possible. If your expenses are more than your income, find ways to cut costs or increase income.

415. Make a list of your needs (rent, food, utility bills, basic phone bills, car payments, insurance, textbooks) and your wants (entertainment, name brand jeans and other clothing, jewelry, eating out, drinking, expensive perfume or toiletries, CDs, electronics, keg parties). Add up the cost of a month's worth of these items and subtract the total from your monthly income. If there's not enough money to go around, start whittling away at the wants, choosing only those that are the most important to you.

416. Be sure to provide for some entertainment in your budget. The idea is to know how much money you have compared to how much you need, not to totally deprive yourself of life's little pleasures. It's all about balance and making wise choices that benefit you the most in the long run. If you totally deny yourself now, you're more likely to splurge in a big way later.

417. Once you've created a budget for the semester, you'll know how much you can afford to spend each week for each expense category. Track your actual expenditures, and if you go over in one category, find ways to cut back in others to make up the difference. If you spend too much early in the semester, you'll end up living on ramen noodles later.

418. When planning your budget, make a few phone calls to find out if there are any fees you may not be aware of that will be added to your tuition bill. Some classes charge extra for course materials or laboratory fees. Being prepared for these additional costs ahead of time can help you avoid a budget shortfall later.

419. Financial aid is usually disbursed at the beginning of each semester, so for a little while you'll feel flush with cash. Don't let this illusion encourage you to overspend. To make your money last, figure out how much you can spend each month and don't exceed this amount.

420. If a month seems like too long a time frame to budget for, divide your monthly income by the number of days in the month and use that as a guideline for how much you can spend each day. If you spend more on the weekend partying or socializing, cut back for a few days until you've made up the difference.

421. Find a budget method that works for you. With the Envelope Method, once you decide on the expense categories you want to track, you place cash in each envelope according to how much you've budgeted for that category for the week or month. When you run out of cash in an envelope, you're done spending money in that category until your next budget period. This low-tech method is a good idea only if you have a secure place to keep the envelopes containing the cash.

422. If the Envelope Method of budgeting doesn't appeal to you, try the Notebook Method, which involves setting up a notebook with a separate page for each of your expense categories. Write the amount you've budgeted for the week or the month for each category. As you spend money, record the purchase in the appropriate category and subtract it from the starting balance to see how much you have left. This method always gives you a quick snapshot of where you stand, but takes daily or weekly recording of your spending.

423. If neither the Notebook Method nor the Envelope Method of budgeting works for you, try the Receipt Method. Keep receipts for each purchase. At the end of the month, total each expense category and compare it to your budget to see where you need to make adjustments. This method requires less frequent recording of your spending but may result in some big unpleasant surprises at the end of the month.

424. Plan ahead for large upcoming expenses. It's easier to save $50 a month than to come up with $200 at once. A little advance planning will give you the peace of mind of knowing you won't be strapped for cash and unable to pay your bills when they're due.

425. Try using personal finance software like Quicken or MS Money, which often comes installed on new computers or can be bought separately, or Mvelopes, a software-based budgeting system. You don't need to use all the bells and whistles, so use only the features you have time for. Just using the checkbook feature will allow you to generate reports showing your spending by category, complete with graphs. Knowing where your money goes can help you control spending.

426. Think of budgeting as a game or a contest that you play against yourself. Make it fun or challenging so you'll stick with it. See how much you can save by cutting costs, and then give yourself a small reward when you do well.

427. If your parents are providing you with spending money, ask them to deposit it in your bank account weekly or monthly. You're on your own for the first time, and it can be hard to resist overspending when you have a big chunk of change in one lump sum. Spend it early and you'll find yourself pleading with Mom and Dad for more dough or living on boxes of mac and cheese.

428. Keep a record of any unexpected expenses you incur. Use this information to update your budget and improve your future expense projections so you have a more realistic picture of your spending and your financial needs.

429. If you look at your expenses on a weekly basis only, you won't get the perspective you need about your spending. Do the math to get a more realistic view. That $25 a week for beer and chips is $1,300 a year! If you're using your credit card to pay for it, add interest to that total. If your job pays $8 an hour, you'd have to work 15 hours a month just to net enough to cover your beer tab.

430. Save money regularly. You may only be able to manage a few dollars a week, but getting in the habit of putting aside money to fall back on in a crunch will serve you well for the rest of your life. If you work, pay yourself first by making a deposit into your savings account before you spend any of the money. If you don't work, set aside a portion of your summer job money or the funds your parents provide.

431. Even students should have an emergency fund. If you can't come up with a big stash all at once, put away as much as you can each week or month until you have $500 or $1,000 that you use only for emergencies. When you have an unplanned expense, like a car repair, you won't have to go into debt and incur interest to pay for it.

432. Save the pennies and the dollars will save themselves. Have you ever saved your change over a period of time and then cashed it in and been surprised at how much you had accumulated? Just as spending small amounts a little bit at a time adds up to significant sums, so does saving small amounts.

433. If you're making an effort to control your spending and you blow your budget in a moment of weakness, don't beat yourself up about it. Buckle down over the next week or several weeks to make up the difference and get back in control.

434. Each week, plan your expenditures for the coming week. Allow yourself some money for entertainment and recreation as well as for food, transportation, and any bills that are due, but make sure you budget within your available funds. Start fresh each week and review everything at the end of the month.

435. It's difficult to manage your money if your paperwork is in a state of disarray. Find a box or use a plastic storage container available at discount stores to set up a simple filing system with folders for Bills to Be Paid, Paid Bills, Financial Aid Information, Bank Accounts, and any other subjects that fit your needs. When bills arrive, open them immediately, check them for accuracy, and stick them in the Bills to Be Paid folder. Go through your folder every week or so to see what needs to be paid.

436. Your family is probably your most important financial resource, and they're probably making sacrifices to send you to college. Don't squander your parents' hard-earned money by spending frivolously or making financial mistakes and expecting them to cover for you. Show your appreciation and respect the contribution they're making to your future by managing your money wisely.

437. Keep receipts for everything you buy. When it's time to update your spending plan (aka, budget), you'll have the receipts to jog your memory.

438. If you don't believe that small amounts can add up to huge sums, think of the episode of *Sex and the City* where Carrie finally did the math and realized she could have bought a condo with the money she'd spent on her collection of Manolo Blahnik designer shoes. It's the small amounts that will get you into trouble because you don't think they matter. That's why recording all your expenses is important. It's the only way to get perspective on your spending.

439. Key areas students can be economical about while in college include food and drink, telephones, and clothing. Does it make sense to spend $20 a week on beer ($80 per month, $720 per school year) or $100 per month ($800 per school year) on long-distance phone charges? Control your spending in these categories and you won't have to borrow as much to get through college.

440. By keeping track of even your small expenditures, you'll better control your spending because you'll be more aware of where your money goes and how quickly the little things add up. It's easy to dribble away hundreds or thousands of dollars, a few dollars at a time, if you don't track your spending on paper or computer.

441. When calculating how much money you'll need to get through a school year, don't forget the cost of getting set up in your dorm room. Most students buy lamps, fans, mini-fridges, microwaves, computer desk and chair, bedding, power strips, extension cords, carpet, an answering machine, and other electronic devices, which can add up to nearly $1,000 in one pop. You don't have to buy it all new. Check out lawn sales and thrift shops and ask your family for donations.

442. Plan for expenses like clothes, toiletries, cosmetics, perfume, and other favorite products. These add up quickly, and if you're used to your parents buying many of these items for you, the price tag may be a shock and you may blow your budget.

443. You'll curb your spending naturally just by tracking what you spend your money on. Awareness helps you make better decisions about the little things that add up to big amounts. If you have no idea that your daily Starbucks habit is costing you $1,100 for the school year (at $4 per day September through May), how will you make smart decisions about the things that matter most to you?

9.

Born to Shop?
Think Again

From the time we're kids, we're bombarded daily
with thousands of advertising and marketing messages. More often than not, we're not even aware
that our thinking and our choices are determined
by these sometimes blatant but often subtle techniques. To make your own independent spending
decisions without the influences of others, you
need to learn to be a savvy consumer.

Be a Savvy Consumer

444. Take a class in marketing. It'll teach you to recognize how advertisers try to influence our thinking and make us want things that may not be good for us or that we don't really need. Being aware of these techniques and recognizing them for what they are can help you resist the temptation to spend for the wrong reasons. Don't let yourself be easily manipulated.

445. Avoid big sale days at the mall or department stores. People buy more when there's a sale, often purchasing things they don't need. If you don't really need it, you didn't really save money on it, no matter how much it was marked down. Even worse, "sale" prices are sometimes more than the regular price because stores first mark up the prices in order to put the items "on sale."

446. When making a major purchase, plan ahead, do your homework, and compare price and quality with other brands and between other stores. Research the product's record in Consumer Reports magazine or read online reviews at reputable sites.

447. Take a long-term view of each of your regular expenses and decide if they're worth the opportunity cost. That $100 a month you drop at the gym costs you $1,200 a year. If you invested that amount at a conservative 6 percent return, you'd have $16,326 in ten years. If you invested it in a tax-deferred retirement account, you'd accumulate over $280,000 by the time you retire. That's opportunity cost.

448. When shopping at the grocery store, check the per-unit price posted next to the total price on the shelf below the item. This will tell you whether it makes more sense to buy a different size or brand. For example, you can tell immediately whether a package of four rolls of paper towel for $4.59 is a better deal than six rolls for $7.00, without having to do the math.

449. Whether you're buying computer equipment, dorm furnishings, or clothing, get in the habit of comparison-shopping. Scout out the prices at several different stores before you buy. Over time, you'll save a significant amount of money. It's a good feeling.

450. Always send in any rebates immediately after you purchase an item. Most people make buying decisions based on rebates but never get around to sending them in.

451. Recognize the impact of advertising on your urge to spend money. You're bombarded daily with advertising messages aimed at convincing you that you can't live without this or that product. Being aware of this can help you resist the urge to splurge.

452. Don't indulge in impulse spending. Plan your purchases ahead of time and don't buy anything you didn't plan on buying. This practice gives you a cooling-down period to decide if an item is something you can afford and really can't live without.

453. Ladies, if you use brand-name department store makeup, switching to drugstore brands while you're in college can save you a lot of money. Lines like Cover Girl, Almay, and similar brands found in drugstores and Wal-Mart offer quality products without the high price tag. Just because department store makeup is more expensive doesn't necessarily mean it's better.

454. Don't fall for hard sales pitches. Signs of an unscrupulous salesperson include: high pressure, insisting that you make a decision immediately, reluctance to provide information about the company, telling you the product is free but requiring you to pay for something in order to get it, a request for your credit card number before you've consented to the sale, or an offer to get your money quickly by picking it up or paying for overnight delivery.

455. Whenever you have an urge to buy something (anything), ask yourself: do I need this (T-shirt, jeans, DVD, CD, sunglasses, or whatever) or do I just want it? If I just want it, is it worth going into debt, increasing the cost due to interest charges, feeling stressed about paying my credit card bill, and possibly having to give up something more important later?

456. Limit your name brand shopping. Name brand clothes are often virtually identical to non-name brand clothes, so splurge a little once in awhile if you want to feel cool, but remember that you're paying for the name, not the quality. A little bit of that goes a long way.

457. Convenience comes at a price. Anytime a vendor has a captive audience, they tend to charge higher prices. This may be true of your campus store or other campus services, so check out prices in town before you buy on campus.

458. When shopping, know the regular price of the item you're looking for so you can tell a bargain from a sales gimmick. Planning your purchases ahead of time instead of buying on impulse gives you the opportunity to research the product, know the regular price, and be able to recognize a bargain.

459. Don't rush to buy the latest electronic gadget. Prices are always higher when new products come on the market. Because technology is changing so rapidly, prices fall fairly quickly, so you shouldn't have to wait long.

460. One of the goals of advertising is to make you feel dissatisfied with what you have. More is not necessarily better, and materialism won't make you happy in the long run, so don't let yourself be manipulated. Resist advertising messages and make your own decisions about buying based on who you are as a person.

461. Car leases can be complex, so unless you understand all the ins and outs, don't lease a car. Car salesmen can make a lease sound like a deal you shouldn't pass up, but they often do so with smoke and mirrors. Bottom line: don't make a decision based solely on the monthly payment. Before considering a lease, read about how to negotiate one with favorable terms and what lease components determine your total cost.

462. If you fall victim to a scam, call your local consumer protection agency. You can find the agency in your state by visiting www.consumeraction.gov/state.shtml. They may be able to help you get your money back, or prevent others from becoming a victim of the same scam.

463. Learn to haggle. Almost anything is negotiable, including credit card interest rates, car prices, long-distance telephone rates, set-up fees, and more. Only one thing is certain: you won't get a better deal if you don't ask.

464. Don't pay to fix things that would cost nearly as much to replace. Basic televisions are a good example. You can buy new ones so cheaply it's usually not worth taking it to a repair shop (we're not talking Plasma TVs here). There's a basic fee just to have it looked at, and you could end up paying more to fix it than it would cost you to replace it with a new one.

465. Look at every deal or offer with a healthy dose of skepticism. If it sounds too good to be true, it probably is. There's no such thing as a $99 airfare to Hawaii, or free shares of Microsoft stock, or a miracle weight loss pill. Check out every offer before pulling out your wallet.

466. Beware of telemarketing scams, which often come in the form of sweepstakes, prize offers, travel deals, investments, requests for charitable donations, work-at-home schemes, magazine sales, lotteries, and business opportunities. Most of these offers can be trashed without further consideration. If you can't resist, check the offer out thoroughly and check with your local Better Business Bureau to see if there have been complaints against the business.

467. Don't use check-cashing services. Why pay a fee to cash a check when you can do it free with a local bank account?

468. When getting prescriptions filled, ask your pharmacist if there's a generic equivalent of the brand-name drug your doctor may have prescribed. In most cases you get the exact same product as the brand-name, minus the big-name pharmaceutical company's advertising costs.

469. Legitimate businesses usually don't send sales pitches via fax, unsolicited email, or phone calls. Ignore those "too good to be true" travel deals that offer your dream vacation at rock bottom prices.

470. When you're planning to make a purchase, check with one or two of the online price search engines like www.pricegrabber.com, www.mysimon.com, or www.bizrate.com. If one or more of the stores they represent carry the product, you'll see a list of the stores and their prices. This is a quick way to find the lowest possible price. If you don't want to use the store with the lowest price because you're not familiar with it, use the lower price as a bargaining tool with a different vendor.

471. Look for outlet or discount stores or those that buy overstocked items or end lots (TJMaxx, Big Lots, Christmas Tree Shops, etc.). You can buy perfectly good stuff at a steep discount. There are also online equivalents of these stores, like www.overstock.com.

472. Buying from catalogs or over the Internet can be costly because you can't always tell the quality or fit of the item you're purchasing until you receive it, and by then your credit card has been charged. Don't let these items hang around in your closet or under your bed. Package them up and send them back for a refund. The few dollars you'll spend on shipping will be worth the credit you'll receive. Make a note to yourself to check to make sure the credit shows up on your next credit card statement.

473. Don't use "retail therapy" as a way to make yourself feel better when you're upset, worried, or depressed. The temporary high you may get from spending money will be long gone when the bills roll in, and there's nothing to deflate your mood more quickly than a bill you can't pay and escalating interest costs. Go on a calming hike outdoors instead.

474. A little advance planning when it comes to gift buying can save you a lot of money. Instead of waiting until just before the holidays or other gift-buying events, shop for gifts throughout the year when you see items on sale and stash them in a safe place until you need them.

475. Before you spend money on the latest software, find out if there's a freeware or shareware version that performs the same function. Freeware is software that can be downloaded free. Shareware creators request a voluntary donation if you like the software after trying it out.

476. Price is not always an indicator of quality. The less expensive cosmetics, store brand canned goods, or less prominent electronics brand may be just as good as the more expensive name brand. Some manufacturers price items higher because it gives them a higher perceived value, but you should make your purchasing decisions based on an intelligent evaluation of products.

477. When an item you use regularly is on sale, stock up on it if storage space allows. You may feel a temporary pinch in your cash flow, but in the long run you'll save money. Don't stock up on things you use only once in a while, though, because the longer it takes you to use up a product, the longer your cash flow will be affected.

478. The first step toward becoming a financially responsible adult is resisting advertising and marketing pitches, which use psychology to make you want their product. Just say "no" to being manipulated like a lab animal. Make conscious buying decisions based on what you need and what you can afford to pay for now.

479. Use eBay to find good deals, but be careful not to get addicted to the bidding process and pay for things you don't really need. When you do find an item you want to buy, make sure the shipping charges won't add so much to the cost that you'd be better off buying the item at the local mall.

480. Instead of buying brand-name over-the-counter drugs like cold remedies and pain relievers, buy generic brands that have the same active ingredients at a much lower cost. Equate is one such off-brand line of products, and your grocery store or drugstore probably have their own line as well.

481. If you take prescription drugs and you don't have a prescription card from your insurer, call around to several local pharmacies to check prices. There's often a big difference from one pharmacy to another. Be sure to check small independent pharmacies as well as the chains because larger doesn't always mean lower prices.

482. Know the difference between cost and cash flow so you won't be short-sighted when shopping for staples like cleaning or paper products. Smaller quantities cost more per item, so spending a little more now will save you money later. For example, buying paper towels by the roll is more expensive per roll than buying a package of twelve rolls. You have to make the cash outlay up front, but you'll pay less per roll by buying more rolls at one time.

483. Avoid buying extended warranties on your electronics or other equipment. Most items come with an adequate manufacturer's warranty, and if there's a manufacturing defect, it's likely to show up within the warranty period. Extended warranties are moneymakers for the business that sells them to you.

484. The less you spend, the less you want. Buying indiscriminately is addictive. Once you put controls on your spending, you'll find the urge to buy stuff weakens and you'll not only have more money, you'll be more content with the things you already have.

485. If you get engaged while you're in college, don't fall for the diamond industry's clever marketing techniques that have convinced millions of Americans that they need to spend a certain amount of their income on a diamond engagement ring. The size of the diamond has nothing to do with the size of your love, and there's no law that says an engagement ring has to be a diamond. Start simple. You can always upgrade after college, when you can better afford it.

486. When you borrow money, ask these questions: What's the interest rate? What are the fees? When the loan is paid off, how much interest will I have paid? If I pay the loan off early, will I pay a penalty? Only when you have the complete picture should you sign on the dotted line.

487. Remember that no purchase is a bargain if it's something you don't really need and wouldn't have bought if it weren't on sale. Getting a $250 leather coat for $100 doesn't save you $150—it costs you $100. Don't kid yourself.

488. Don't give out your bank account information over the telephone to a person you don't know. All a scam artist needs to withdraw all the money from your account is your name, bank account number, and routing number. Scam artists devise clever schemes for getting you to provide this information over the phone. Be cautious and skeptical.

489. Don't make a purchase online unless you're sure the site is secure. Watch for the padlock icon on the status bar at the bottom of your browser window to turn to the locked position, and the "http" in your address bar to turn to "https" when you go to the payment section (before you enter your credit card information). These two changes indicate that the site is secure. If you don't see these, don't enter your credit card information; your credit card number could be stolen and used without your knowledge.

490. Make sure you download the most recent version of your browser to take advantage of the most up-to-date security features and advances in encryption capabilities to protect you from Internet fraud. Hackers are constantly finding ways to get around security features in browsers; so staying current is the only way to avoid being a victim.

491. Before submitting personal information to a website, read their privacy policy to find out how the information may be used and whether it will be sold or shared with other businesses. If you don't like what you read, shop somewhere else.

492. Use a credit card, not a debit card, for Internet purchases. Debit cards don't have the same legal protection as credit cards when it comes to limiting your liability for fraudulent use. Your bank accounts could be wiped out and you would have no legal recourse.

493. Practice safe online shopping. Shop only on sites you're familiar with and only make transactions you've initiated.

494. Never, ever buy anything from a site you learned about from spam email. Spam spreads viruses to millions of computers, costing consumers millions of dollars, but it's still around because some people respond to it. If fewer people respond, spam emails will end, along with the viruses that often go with them.

495. If you need a computer for college, you don't need to buy all the bells and whistles just because they're available. Nearly any new computer on the market today comes equipped with the features you'll need, unless you're majoring in a field like engineering or graphic design, which require intense processing capabilities. If money is an issue, you can get by without a DVD ROM drive, high-end sound system, and larger size or flat-screen monitor. You can also cut costs by buying 128 to 256 MB of RAM versus 528, a 600–800 Mhz processor instead of 1.3 Ghz, and a 20 GB hard drive instead of 40 GB or greater. Equipping your computer to use it as an entertainment center (playing DVD movies, 3-D video games, etc.) will significantly increase your costs, but the basics will do just fine for your course work requirements.

496. Before you buy a computer, check with your college. Some schools provide laptops to students as part of the price of tuition. If yours is one of them, there's no sense in spending your own money on a duplicate piece of equipment.

497. Nowadays, most college students have their own computers, but if money is especially tight, for the price of a little inconvenience, you can shave $1,000 to $2,000 off your expenses by using the computers in the school's computer lab.

498. Your college may require you to have a computer that contains certain components. For example, you may be required to have wireless Internet capability. Before you buy a computer, check with the school regarding their requirements and suggestions. It's more expensive to add capabilities after the fact.

499. Before you buy a new computer to take to college, check with your campus bookstore to see if they offer student discounts on computer equipment. Most do, and you could save as much as 25 percent or more off retailer's prices.

10.

Miscellaneous Money-Saving Tips

College campuses can be a money booby trap, with hidden fees, fines, surprise charges, temptations, needs, and wants. Most students struggle financially to stretch their money to cover the essentials and still have fun. Using simple or creative money-saving ideas to cut costs in some areas can make it possible for you to afford some of the indulgences that are important to you.

500. If you're furnishing an apartment, check into homebuilders' model home closeouts. Builders often auction off quality model home furniture at a tenth of its cost new when they've sold the last houses or lots in a development.

501. Many college bills include athletic fees. If you don't play a sport and don't plan to use the athletic facilities, see if you can get the fee waived. Why pay for something you won't use?

502. If there's a beauty school in your town, have your hair cut there. Beauty school students learn the latest styles and techniques and are supervised by professionals. The schools charge a much lower fee than regular hair salons.

503. Keep track of your dorm room key. Replacements will cost you $30 or more.

504. Avoid book or CD clubs by mail. They start out cheap but get more expensive. If you forget to send in your form each month declining the CD or book of the month, you'll end up spending a lot of money on something you might not even have wanted.

505. Skip the tanning booth. A tan is not a sign of good health, as so many people believe. It's a sign of overexposure to ultraviolet light that causes skin cancer, premature aging of the skin, and damage to your immune system, not to mention a thinning of your wallet. Get sun in moderation the natural way: outdoors.

506. Clever marketing may have convinced you that expensive shampoos work better than inexpensive ones, but studies have shown otherwise. That $10 shampoo you buy at the hair salon does no more for your hair than the $3 supermarket variety. Try a few inexpensive brands until you find one you really like.

507. Think of eating out at restaurants as a luxury and plan accordingly. Like most things, if you do it all the time, you'll take it for granted. A habit of eating out regularly can be one of your biggest budget busters.

508. You can spend an exorbitant amount of money on grooming without realizing it. Add up the cost of perms, highlighting or coloring, salon haircuts and trims, manicures and pedicures, brand-name makeup, perfume, lotions, special shampoos…the list goes on. Try reducing costs by having a friend give you a manicure or pedicure and help you color or highlight your hair. Buy less expensive toiletries and makeup, which are often just as good as the name brand products.

509. Adopt a simpler hairstyle that doesn't require frequent trimming in order to look good. Getting your hair trimmed every three to four months instead of every month could save you $250 to $600 or more a year. Getting less frequent perms can double that savings.

510. Don't waste big bucks on a wide assortment of cleaning supplies. Baking soda and vinegar can do almost any cleaning job just as well as the expensive store-bought cleaners, for a fraction of the cost.

511. Just because you have a car at school doesn't mean you have to use it everywhere you go. Walk or bike whenever possible. You'll feel more energetic, stay fitter, and save money on gas, parking, and wear and tear on your car. Save the car for longer trips, grocery shopping, or bad weather.

512. Learn to wield a needle and thread well enough to sew on a button, hem a pair of pants, or fix a small tear. Otherwise you'll waste money buying new clothes you don't really need just because of a minor problem like a loose button.

513. Limit your online shopping. When you make a purchase online, record it in your check register or on a log of credit card purchases so you can keep track of how much you've spent that month. Online purchases can become addictive because you don't feel like you're spending real money, and they can add up very quickly. Keeping a list provides a reality check.

514. Use your computer to make greeting cards. Most computers come with free programs that can be used to make all sorts of cards, or you can buy greeting card software (a one-time purchase), or use clip-art or original photos and create your own images for the cards. You'll have fun, receive compliments on your creativity, and save $2.00 to $4.00 per card.

515. If you have access to a hose, wash your car yourself instead of going to a car wash. If you don't have access to a hose, use a do-it-yourself car wash instead of the full-service type.

516. If you really can't stomach tap water, buy spring water by the gallon and pour it into a smaller bottle. If you drink one 16 ounce container of bottled water a day, you could save 25 percent, or $25 a month or more.

517. Don't buy books that you're going to read for pleasure. Use the library, swap with friends, or go to used book sales or yard sales. People are always trying to get rid of per-fectly good books. Limit purchases to books you want to keep for reference, like a good dictionary and thesaurus.

518. If you're a camera hound, get a digital camera and upload your favorite photos to an online service like www.ofoto.com for printing. Not only will you save the cost of film at $4.00 or more per roll, you won't keep paying for photos that don't come out well.

519. Buy school supplies like paper, pencils, and pens at an odd-lot store like Big Lots. They buy leftover items at a steep discount and pass the savings on to you. Why pay full price for the same product?

520. Crime has become big business on college campuses because today's students bring so many valuables to school with them: computers (many of them fully portable and easy to steal), DVD and CD players, electronic games, Palm Pilots, and other gadgets. Keep track of your stuff, keep your dorm room or apartment locked, and keep valuables out of sight.

521. When you hang out with people who spend money freely, it's tempting to do the same. Resist the urge to keep up with your friends' and roommates' spending. They may have more money than you do, or they may be getting more deeply in debt.

522. Cosigning a loan for anyone, even your best friend or someone you're dating, is a bad idea. You'll be responsible for paying the loan if your friend fails to make a payment. Although you believe your friend would never leave you holding the bag, it happens every day to people who thought the same thing.

523. Invoices from your college can rival a hospital bill for complexity and sheer length, and you should check them over just as carefully. You may find items that shouldn't be charged to you or that are for the wrong amount. Go to the bursar's office and ask for an explanation of any items you don't understand or that seem incorrect.

524. Don't blow your income tax refund. Use it to cover some of your mandatory expenses (like textbooks), pay off your credit card balance, or start (or add to) your emergency fund. It's a shame to fritter it away instead of using it in a way that will give you the most bang for your buck.

525. If you're having sex, or planning to, protect yourself. Condoms and other birth control methods are cheap and convenient compared to the cost of raising a child or paying child support for the next eighteen years. Safe-sex organizations on campus or Planned Parenthood often offer free condoms.

526. Before you head off to college, have "the talk" with your parents—not the birds and the bees talk, but the money talk. Discuss your expectations and their expectations related to who is paying for what. You don't want to spend a bunch of money on the assumption that your parents are going to be providing a certain amount, only to find that they're not, and you've blown your cash on something you could have done without.

527. Shakespeare knew what he was talking about when he said "neither a borrower nor a lender be." Don't lend money to friends, roommates, or classmates. You may never get it back, which can cause bad feelings and permanently damage your relationship.

528. Set up a file folder labeled "receipts" and place all your receipts for major purchases in it. If something goes wrong with an item, you may be able to get it fixed or exchanged under warranty. If you don't have your receipt, you'll have to pay for the repair.

529. Income tax refund loans (instant refunds) give you access to your money more quickly, but they're a consumer rip-off, with annual percentage interest rates as high as 775 percent. It doesn't make sense to pay such exorbitant interest rates just to get your refund a week or so sooner. You can achieve the same result by filing online and having your refund deposited directly into your checking account.

530. Never sign anything without reading every word of it. If you don't understand something in the document, ask for an explanation. Very few people read what they sign, and many of them end up getting the short end of the stick. The few minutes it takes you to carefully read the small print could save you money and hassles.

531. Don't leave your car keys in the ignition or in any conspicuous place, like the glove box. It's an invitation to have your car stolen, or at the very least to have your CD collection pilfered.

532. If you begin to fall into financial trouble, talk to your parents before you get in too deeply. It's easier (and less costly) to prevent money problems from escalating than it is to clear them up, and your parents have been handling money for many years. You should be able to benefit from their experience.

533. If you have an Individual Retirement Account (IRA), you can withdraw money from it without penalty if the money is used for higher education expenses. This might be a better choice for you than paying interest on a bank loan.

534. Before consolidating your debts, make sure you've considered the long-term costs. Most consolidations end up costing you more in the long-term because you roll long- and short-term loans together and extend the due date, which increases interest costs.

535. Regularly review the activity on your school-related accounts, such as the bookstore and cafeteria, to make sure nobody has used your account or meal plan without authorization. If you spot anything suspicious or questionable, contact your school immediately.

536. If you work while you're in college, put aside a set amount of money, preferably at least 10 percent, from each paycheck into a savings account, even if you think you can't afford to. If you get in the habit of paying yourself first, after a short time you won't even notice that the money is gone, and you'll save a nice little cushion to fall back on when you really need it.

537. If it sounds too good to be true, it probably is. If you receive an offer that makes you the least bit suspicious, don't respond to it. If you want to satisfy your curiosity about an email offer (like the one that circulated on the Internet about free shares of Microsoft stock), look it up on urbanlegends.about.com to see if it's legitimate.

538. Gift cards are great, but if you don't use them within a year, most stores deduct a fee. Use the card promptly, and if you don't really want it, swap it online for a different card of the same value at another store by visiting www.swapagift.com. You can also sell it, but you won't get full value.

539. If you find yourself temporarily short of funds for rent, food, or other living expenses, rather than taking a credit card cash advance or a short-term bank loan, ask your financial aid office if they can help. Many schools have funds available for short-term interest-free loans of $500 to $800 to get you through a tight spot while waiting for a financial aid disbursement or other funds to arrive.

540. Take advantage of campus health services. There's probably no cheaper or more convenient health care available to you.

541. If you lose your checkbook or find checks missing, report the loss to your bank immediately to protect yourself from misuse by a thief. The bank will be responsible for cashing any forged checks on your account, but only if you report the checks missing as soon as you know.

542. Use all other alternatives available to you, like reducing expenses and increasing income, before consolidating loans (excluding student loans). It's too easy to borrow more than you really need, and it allows you to continue living beyond your means, merely postponing the inevitable moment when you realize you are in over your head.

543. If you're having trouble paying your bills because the due dates fall between paychecks, call your creditors and ask to have the due date of your bill changed so it arrives at a more convenient time. This could prevent late fees, which not only use up your cash but also cause black marks on your credit record.

544. Keep your bills and the accompanying envelopes for submitting payments in a safe spot. Your creditor may require you to use the preprinted envelope they provided. If you don't, the payment could take several extra days to be credited to your account and you could incur a late charge (as high as $39 for late credit card payments).

545. If you have a stored value card or gift card, guard it carefully. These cards are usually not protected by law so you won't get your money back if yours is stolen or used without your authorization.

546. Plan well in advance to make sure all your classes will be available when you need them. This will give you time to juggle your schedule to make sure you fit in those classes that aren't offered every semester. Otherwise you may find yourself paying for an extra semester or two—a very expensive proposition.

547. Read the fine print on all the documents your college sends you. The costs won't necessarily be in bold print, and fees can add up.

548. Stay away from what is commonly referred to as payday loans, where you borrow a certain amount of money for a short period (usually a week or two, until payday) for a fee. You give the payday loan company a personal check for the borrowed amount plus the fee, and they give you the cash. They hold onto the check until the agreed upon time. The annual percentage rate (APR) on these loans is obscene, usually several hundred percent, and sometimes several thousand percent.

549. You may feel you don't have enough time to go to school full-time, study, and hold down a job, but studies show that students who work a moderate amount (not full-time) during college actually do better academically. Juggling work and school requires discipline and planning that pays off in all areas of your life.

550. Do you have stuff to ship from home to school or vice versa? Greyhound (the bus company) offers students up to 50 percent off its regular Greyhound PackageXpress shipping services for same day and overnight delivery of oversized or heavy packages.

551. Squirrel away some coins in your car in case you need cash. If you don't smoke, keep change in your ashtray so it's handy when you need to pay a toll or feed a parking meter. It could keep you from getting an expensive parking ticket.

552. If you're sending a package, prepare it yourself and take it to the U.S. Post Office instead of using one of those mailing services like Mail It 4U, which are convenient but tack on a substantial fee. The U.S. Post Office has a good selection of reasonably priced packaging materials, including envelopes and boxes. Some of them are even free.

553. Save money by using smaller amounts of product than the packaging recommends. You can do this with shampoo, dish detergent or dishwasher soap, laundry detergent, fabric softener, and cleaning products without any noticeable loss of results. Experiment to find an amount that does the job without wasting the product.

554. If your school offers a reloadable card that can be used on campus for meals or in the campus store, take advantage of it. You pay up front, your ID card is loaded with a set dollar amount, and you use it on campus like a debit card. You don't have to carry cash around with you that might be lost or stolen or that you might be tempted to spend on something else.

555. With most things in life, attitude is everything. Develop an attitude of being willing to do without for the few years you're in college. You'll feel less deprived when you can't afford the latest electronic gadget or expensive spring break, and you'll have less student loan money or credit card debt to repay after graduation.

556. How you handle your money in college is a precursor to how you're likely to handle your money after you graduate. Avoiding bad spending or credit habits now will make life after graduation easier and help you achieve your financial goals.

557. Avoid situations that trigger impulse spending: malls, certain stores, shopping with friends who spend lavishly, or shopping when you're sad or depressed. You'll be paying for your impulse for months.

558. Don't hang out at the mall. It encourages impulse spending or using shopping as a form of recreation. Find another way to spend your free time and only go to the mall when you're ready to make a planned purchase.

559. Instead of equipping your own mini-office in your dorm room, take advantage of staplers, hole punches, disks, paper clips, and other supplies at your campus library. All it takes is a little advance planning to save a few dollars.

560. You'll go through lots of pens and pencils during your college career, so be on the lookout for freebies from businesses, organizations, and banks. Many businesses also give out free notepads, sticky-notes, and other office supplies with their logo on them. Collect these and you won't have to spend as much money on supplies.

561. Shop sparingly for Christmas. Your friends and family know you're trying to put yourself through college. They don't expect you to spend lots of money on them, so a token gift is all that's necessary.

562. You won't always have your parents to bail you out from the consequences of your financial decisions, but if you're really in trouble, phone home. Your parents might prefer to advance you some cash rather than see you take on credit card debt with high interest rates. The cost to you: listening politely to any ensuing lecture.

563. If you come across a good deal that seems legit, that doesn't mean you should go for it. Ask yourself if it's important in the overall scheme of things. Do you really need to belong to a CD club? Always read the small print (there's a reason it's small—they'd rather you didn't read it).

564. Many colleges have their own version of "Dump and Run," a type of giant yard sale where students leaving campus for the summer, or for good, dump unwanted furniture, appliances, clothes, books, and household goods. You can buy much of what you need to set up house in the dorm or in an apartment at a fraction of the cost you'd pay at even the best discount store.

565. Take advantage of the free perks your school has to offer. Instead of joining a health club or gym, use the campus facilities, which often include state-of-the-art racquetball courts, tennis courts, gyms, and weight-training equipment. You're also more likely to stick to your exercise program when you use facilities right on campus where you spend most of your time.

566. It makes sense to use free services when possible rather than spending your own money. Remember that libraries carry more than just books. Borrow videos, DVDs, CDs, and audio tapes from the campus or town library rather than buying them.

567. Do the burger flippers at the local fast-food restaurants know you by name? If eating out is a lifestyle instead of a treat, try cutting back. It's much more expensive than shopping at the grocery store and preparing your own simple meals, and more fattening.

568. Check out the local dollar store for common household items like cleaning and office supplies, greeting cards, candles, drinking glasses, dishes, photo frames, gift-wrap, and other odds and ends. These stores are a bargain hunter's paradise.

569. Don't let down your guard when it comes to controlling your spending just because you're flush with cash from your summer job. Continue to practice the same control you've practiced during the school year and save as much of your earnings as possible. Every dollar saved is a dollar less you have to borrow with interest.

570. When tempted to spend money, calculate how many hours you'd have to work to earn after taxes to pay the purchase price. If you work during the school year or summer and earn $9 per hour, your after-tax income might be around $7 per hour. You'd have to work two-and-a-half hours to pay for a new CD, or 214 hours to pay for a $1,500 spring break tab. Is it worth it?

571. Save money on gifts by performing a service instead of buying a product. Offer free babysitting, a massage, or lawn care. Create a photo album. Wash the car. Bake goodies. Use your imagination to come up with a creative gift.

572. Scam artists love to target students. One of the most prolific areas for student scams is spring break and other travel, so be especially cautious when using these services.

573. Take only the amount of cash out of the bank that you really need for your daily expenses. Leave the rest in the bank and leave your ATM card at home. Having to work a little harder to have access to your cash makes you less likely to impulse shop or overspend.

574. Go natural: wear the hair color you were born with. If you really feel you must color your hair, do it yourself or have a friend do it for you. Having your hair colored at the beauty salon can cost between $400 and $600 per school year if you have to have it touched up every month or so. Doing it yourself costs around $70 per school year.

575. Instead of blowing "found" money like bonuses, rebates, overtime pay, and cash gifts from family, put them in your savings account and use them to cover school essentials. You'll reduce the amount you have to borrow and the interest you'll have to pay.

576. Don't be afraid to admit to your friends that you can't afford to spend money on entertainment or other discretionary expenses. Finishing your degree with a minimum of debt is your number one goal, and that's nothing to be embarrassed about.

577. Don't gamble! It's expensive recreation and can turn into addiction.

578. Start a barter club on campus or join one in your community. These clubs allow people to swap items they no longer need for something they do need, or to trade services without any money exchanging hands. It's a great way to recycle and save money. To get started and find a group near you, visit www.freecycle.org, a global online swap group with many local member groups.

579. When sending mail, use the smallest envelope or packaging possible, weigh the package, and use the appropriate amount of postage. Why pad the pockets of the U.S. Postal Service?

580. If you buy something every time you feel the urge, you'll graduate knee-deep in debt. Learn to ignore the urge to splurge. Make planned, conscious spending choices and remember that a little sacrifice builds character and your bank account.

581. Forego tattoos and body piercings while you're in college. You have more important uses for your money. If you still want the body art after graduation when you're earning your own money and paying your own way, go for it.

582. Get rid of your AOL account. Internet access is free at many colleges, but it doesn't include AOL. You'll enjoy experiencing the Internet without the restrictions and parameters set by your Internet service. The good news is that you can still use AOL Instant Messenger for free.

583. Save money by staying healthy. Colds and the flu make the rounds of college dorms and classrooms throughout the winter. Getting sick not only makes you fall behind in your studies, it can cost considerable money in throat lozenges, cough syrup, cold tablets, tissues, decongestants, and maybe even doctor visits. Most illnesses are spread by hand, so wash your hands often.

584. Instead of buying an expensive dictionary and thesaurus, use online versions, like Merriam Webster (www.m-w.com). They're quick and easy, and best of all, free.

585. New jewelry is one thing that you can definitely do without during college, yet it's one of the top spending categories for college women. Keep your perspective about what's important during your college years. Reward yourself with a nice piece of jewelry after you graduate and are making money, instead of using money provided by your parents, the U.S. government, or your school in the form of financial aid.

586. Don't drop $100 or more for a pair of sunglasses. Expensive shades don't necessarily offer greater protection than inexpensive ones. Know what protection you need and make sure you get it, but paying more than $20 for something that's fragile and easily lost or scratched doesn't make sense for a student.

587. Talk to upper classmen and ask for tips on making the most of your money in college. They've been there, done that. Why not learn from their experience and spare yourself the aggravation of learning the hard way?

588. You have the big ticket items like tuition and room and board covered, but you may be surprised by how quickly the incidentals add up. Laundry, fees related to your major (lab fees, art supplies), pens, pencils, paper, printer cartridges, and toiletries add up to quite a sum. When developing your budget, be sure to include an allowance for these items or you may overspend in other areas and run out of money before the end of the semester.

589. Skip the campus bookstore when buying office supplies like pens, pencils, paper, and computer disks. You'll save money by buying these supplies at discount office supply stores like Staples or Office Depot, or at a discount odd lots store.

590. It may sound like a radical idea, but be open-minded: consider leaving your car at home. A car is usually unnecessary if you live on campus, and you could save thousands of dollars a year on gas, insurance, maintenance, campus parking permits, and the inevitable parking tickets.

591. Don't waste your money on souvenirs: baseball caps, T-shirts, sweatshirts, cheap trinkets from beach shops, or other stuff you'll put aside and forget about. If you want a memento from a place you visited and really loved, buy an inexpensive poster, print, or postcard that will remind you of the good time you had there.

592. When planning your courses, be aware that some classes aren't offered every semester, or you may have conflicts that prohibit you from taking two classes you need at the same time. If you don't plan carefully, you may end up having to spend an additional semester or two in order to finish your degree requirements. More semesters equal more money. Lots more money.

593. At the end of the year, turn in your dorm room key. If you forget, you'll be billed $100 to $150 for changing the locks.

594. If you're underage, don't drink in the dorms. In some towns, undercover police cruise the dorms looking for instances of under aged drinking because of the high crime rates associated with it. If you get caught, you'll be slapped with hefty fines (hundreds of dollars) and be required to do community service. You could even be arrested and hauled off to jail. Now that's a phone call you won't want to make to your parents.

595. Keep track of your driver's license. If you lose it, you'll have to pay $20 to $40 to get a new one issued.

596. If you need computer equipment, furniture, electronics, or housewares, regularly check the classified ads in your local newspapers and the campus bulletin board. You can easily find perfectly good items for a fraction of what you'd pay new.

597. Shopping at Goodwill and other thrift stores has become the thing to do. You can often find cool, quality clothing and furnishings in good condition at steeply reduced prices. Many items are new or nearly new, and in upscale neighborhoods, you may even find designer clothes for a couple of dollars.

598. Read magazines at the library instead of buying them. Three or four magazines could add up to $12 to $15 per month, or $180 a year. If you must buy, make a deal with a roommate or friend to swap magazines so you don't both buy the same ones.

599. Save money by sharing a printer with your roommate. Work out a fair deal so that the person who actually bought the printer gets reimbursed over time for part of the initial investment, and share the cost of ink cartridges.

600. You may also be able to avoid buying a printer by using the school's equipment. Save your documents on a disk or CD and print them out at the computer lab.

601. If you work, sign up for direct deposit of your paycheck. You're much less likely to spend your money impulsively if it goes directly into your checking account. Some banks also charge lower fees if you use direct deposit.

602. Don't subscribe to fee-based Internet sites unless they provide information you need for your courses and you can't get the information anywhere else. A few dollars here and there add up over the course of a semester or school year. Game and quiz sites hook lots of young people, but is it really worth $9.95 a month to be able to take quizzes like "What kind of kisser are you?" or "What's your dating IQ?"

603. Don't waste your money on diet aids like pills, candies, or similar products. Americans spend an estimated $6 billion a year on fraudulent or ineffective diet products, but the only way to lose weight is to exercise and eat less. If you have a weight problem, your money would be better spent consulting a doctor.

604. Keep foremost in your mind that your main focus in college is studying, learning, and getting good grades so you can get a better job when you graduate. Spend less in college and you'll have to work less. You'll have more time to study and get the education and grades that will help you earn the big bucks later.

605. One of the most important money-saving lessons you can learn is to delay gratification. You don't have to have everything you want right now. Delaying gratification means giving up some things now so you can get a good education and earn more money later without being burdened with credit card debt.

606. Being on your own doesn't mean you can do everything you want, now that Mom and Dad aren't there to question you. Being an adult means making choices—sometimes tough ones—about how to spend your money. If you indulge every whim, you'll end up paying much more for it later in the form of high interest expenses.

607. Tuition is only part of the story when it comes to paying for college. Don't underestimate the costs of your social life, books, food, rent, fees, transportation, clothes, and shoes. Most students don't realize how much money their parents spend on these items, and it can be a rude awakening to suddenly be responsible for paying for them yourself.

608. To trick yourself into saving money, pay for everything with paper money and save all your change. Each day, empty your purse or pockets and put all the change in a big jar. You'll never miss it. When the jar is full, turn the change in at the bank. It's an easy way to build a savings account.

609. Keep track of the dates your bills are due by marking them on a calendar. This tickler system will help ensure that you don't incur late charges and will help keep your credit history healthy.

610. Avoid window-shopping, cruising the mall, and browsing aimlessly through online storefronts. If you constantly face temptation, you'll eventually give in to the impulse to buy something you don't need and would never have set out to buy deliberately.

611. One of the best things you can do for your bank account is quit smoking. A pack-a-day habit at $4 per pack doesn't sound like much, but it totals $1,440 a year. If you saved that money and earned 6 percent a year on it, you'd have over $19,000 in ten years and over $336,000 by retirement.

612. Train yourself to go through this thought process when you're tempted to make a purchase: Do I really need or want this item? If yes, can it wait? If no, do I already have something similar that will work, or can I borrow the item? If no, do I want this item badly enough to take the money from my long-term goals? If yes, can I buy a similar item that costs less?

613. It may seem obvious, but don't buy anything you don't need. You can buy things for pleasure after you graduate and are earning your own way. For now, buy only what you need.

614. Focus on your short- and long-term goals regularly. You'll be less tempted to spend money on things you don't really need.

615. If you need motivation to take control of your spending while you're in college, think about the latest trend of college graduates moving back in with Mom and Dad after graduation because they have so much debt they can't afford to live on their own. Sure you love your parents, but do you want to live with them again after being out on your own for four years?

11.

Live Thrifty Now

It's always possible to find ways to do things less expensively, and it can actually be fun to be thrifty, especially when frugality in some areas allows you to splurge in others and still live within your means. The higher the cost of a service or product, the more opportunity you have to save money, so housing, food, and utilities are ripe for a little painless cost-cutting.

616. Dorm living can be very cost effective, but don't automatically assume it'll be cheaper to live in the dorms. Your school may require you to live on campus your freshman year, but after that, you may want to check out the costs of a shared apartment off campus. Don't forget to factor in all the costs, including rent, utilities, parking, and transportation. Also consider the up front cash outlay for security deposits, first and last months' rent, and utility deposits.

617. Get free housing and maybe even a free meal ticket by becoming a Resident Assistant or Residential Advisor (RA) during your junior and senior years. You'll play a leadership role in your dorm building and gain valuable experience in addition to the free ride. Only responsible students need apply.

618. To defray the costs of room and board, look into co-operative (co-op) housing, where a group of students (often with something in common such as an ethnic, religious, cultural, or other interests) share living quarters and prepare meals as a group. This type of housing is not only fun and educational; it can be cheaper than living on campus or in an off-campus apartment. You could save up to 50 percent on your housing costs.

619. Before choosing your campus housing, find out all of the alternatives and what each one costs. Don't assume that all on-campus housing costs the same. You may be able to save money by living in a smaller room or by living in a space that has three roommates instead of two.

620. If you live in an apartment or co-op off campus, your parents' homeowners insurance policy probably won't cover your stuff. If that's the case, you may want to buy renters insurance, which covers your possessions from damage by smoke, fire, water, and other perils, as well as theft or vandalism, and protects you from liability if someone sues you because they were hurt in your apartment.

621. Do your homework before deciding to move to an apartment off campus. There are more costs, and certainly more potential liabilities, than you may be aware of, so make your decision based on all the facts.

622. It doesn't sound as exciting as living in the dorms, but you can save a lot of money by living at home while attending college. If money is tight, consider living at home for the first year or two. When it comes time to start paying off your student loans, you'll be glad you did because your student loans will be tens of thousands of dollars less.

623. If you rent an apartment off campus, financial experts recommend that you pay no more than 25 to 30 percent of your income for rent. The only way to know how much you can afford is to do a budget before you commit to a lease.

624. If you decide you can save money by moving off campus, look for an apartment on your own or use free assistance provided by your college rather than using a realtor or apartment locator service. You'll save at least the equivalent of one month's rent, which is the fee most locator services charge. In some cities, you could save even more than a month's rent.

625. If you decide to try living off campus, investigate the costs thoroughly and make sure you know exactly what will be required of you. Read all the fine print in the lease to avoid unpleasant surprises later.

626. If you live off campus, you may be responsible for paying your own heating costs. Depending on what region of the country you live in, these costs could be substantial. Find ways to conserve energy to lower your heating bills.

627. Lots of energy is lost through glass windows and doors. If you don't have curtains on your windows, consider installing some energy-efficient window coverings. They'll help keep the space warmer in winter and cooler in summer, reducing your heating and cooling costs.

628. Don't heat areas you don't use everyday. Close registers in unused rooms and leave the doors to the unheated rooms closed.

629. Don't run the bathroom ventilation fan in the winter while you're taking a shower or using the bathroom. If you must use it, leave it on for as short a time as possible. A bathroom fan can suck all the heated air out of the average house in little more than an hour. With three or four roommates showering every day, the fan can significantly increase your heating costs.

630. Keep your thermostat set between sixty-four and sixty-eight degrees while you're home and between sixty and sixty-four degrees when you're not home. There's no sense in heating the house or apartment when nobody is there.

631. Don't turn the thermostat way up so the house or room will warm up faster. It doesn't work that way. Set it at the desired temperature, not above.

632. Open your blinds or curtains on the sunny side of the house in winter to take advantage of solar energy to help heat your living space. When the sun goes down, close the blinds or curtains to help retain the solar heat.

Consider the Hidden Costs of Living Off Campus

633. Before deciding to live in an apartment, you should be aware that you'd usually be required to pay the first and last month's rent up front, plus a security deposit equal to at least one month's rent. Can your cash flow situation handle this much cash tied up indefinitely?

634. When you move off campus, you'll probably be required to pay utility deposits in order to have the electricity, water, oil or gas, and trash removal switched over to your name. Be prepared to cough up the cash for these deposits in addition to the rent and security deposits. Call the utility companies in advance and find out how much you'll be required to deposit.

635. If you have a car, you may be required to pay for parking at your off-campus apartment. Depending on the city or town, the fees can be significant, so be sure to ask about this when checking out apartments.

636. If your off-campus apartment prohibits smoking and your landlord finds out that you smoked while living there, you could forfeit your security deposit. Think twice before trying to pull the wool over the landlord's eyes.

637. If you plan to have a pet, find an apartment that officially allows them. You may have to make a pet deposit in case your pet damages the apartment, but it will be cheaper than forfeiting your entire security deposit if a pet is not allowed and you're caught having one.

638. Consider renters insurance, which will protect your belongings if they're stolen or damaged by fire. For some students, this coverage may not make sense, but if you have a lot of money tied up in computers, other electronics, jewelry, or an expensive wardrobe, it's worth paying for.

639. Before signing an apartment lease, read all the fine print. Long, boring documents often contain surprises that can cost you a lot of money, and this is especially true of housing leases.

640. When looking for housing, find out if your school has any campus-owned apartments. They have advantages over privately owned apartments because they're usually safer, cleaner, and kept in better repair. A big plus is that the lease for a campus-owned apartment terminates at the end of the semester. Privately owned apartment leases are usually for a full year, which means you have to find someone to sublet the apartment when you leave for the summer, or pay the rent yourself even though you're not living there.

641. Many students believe it's cheaper to live off campus, but studies don't always bear this out. Students tend to underestimate the costs associated with living in an off-campus apartment, which include rent, electricity, water, heat, phone, cable TV, and trash removal. If you're thinking of moving off campus to save money, get all the facts to make sure it will really be cheaper than living on campus.

642. At the end of your apartment lease, turn in your keys. You may be charged extra rent after the ending date of the lease if you delay, or you could be charged a fee for having the locks changed.

643. Ask your college if you'll be assessed a nonresident fee if you move off campus. If so, factor this into your cost analysis when determining whether living off campus will save you money.

644. When calculating the cost of living off campus, be sure to consider the cost of commuting. Will you walk or bike to classes every day, even in the rain or snow? Will you need to pay for a bus pass? Will you be tempted to take a taxi in bad weather? Be realistic.

645. If you live off campus, you'll be required to pay your rent and security deposit up front, but your financial aid funds will not be available until the first day of classes. Plan ahead and make sure you'll have other funds available to cover these payments without your financial aid.

646. Obviously, it's a lot cheaper to live off campus if you share expenses with roommates. Protect yourself by making sure that each roommate's name is on the lease and on the utility accounts so you don't risk being stuck with all the liability if someone doesn't pay up. It happens all the time, even among friends.

647. When you rent an off-campus apartment with other roommates, it's in your best interest to be sure they're going to be able to pay their share of the rent, utilities, and other expenses. If they're unable to pay, you could be stuck with their share of the costs in addition to your own. Ask each potential roommate about how they expect to pay their share, and if you're not satisfied with the answer, think twice about moving in together.

648. When you live in the dorms, basic furniture is provided and included in your fees. When you live off campus, you'll have to come up with much of your own furniture, as well as lamps, dishes, pots and pans, kitchen appliances, rugs, and other household items. Buying them at the annual "Dump and Run" or a thrift store like Goodwill can reduce the cost, but you should still plan on needing to spend a chunk of change to set up house.

649. If you rent an apartment with others, and any utilities (electric, phone, gas, etc.) are in your name, close out the accounts when you move, and let the roommates you're leaving behind set up their own accounts. Don't let a roommate assume responsibility if the bill is in your name. If the person doesn't pay the bills on time, you'll be held responsible for the payments, and it could ruin your credit score.

650. Pay your rent late and your landlord could charge you a hefty late fee. Most leases spell out the amount for late fees and how late you can be before the fee is charged. Read your lease.

651. If you move out of your apartment before your lease is up, you may lose all or part of your security deposit. What's worse, your landlord can legally make you pay the rent through the end of the lease even if you're no longer living in the apartment. Plan ahead to avoid this waste of money.

652. If your parents are financially able to purchase a house in your college town as an investment, you could get free housing and charge other students rent that would cover the costs of ownership. Look for a house within walking distance to campus with as many bedrooms as possible for the best investment.

653. If you can find ways to cut rent, one of your largest expenses, you'll end up owing less on student loans or credit cards when you graduate. Either live at home as long as possible, look for a free room in someone's house in exchange for helping with yard work, housecleaning, or childcare, or live in a co-op or group apartment.

654. If you don't leave your dorm room or apartment in pristine condition when you move out, you'll lose your deposit at the end of the semester. Don't give your landlord an excuse to keep your money. Clean thoroughly, including carpets, and repair anything you break. A couple of hours of your time will help ensure you get your deposit back.

655. Breaking your lease early can be expensive. You can be held responsible for paying the rent for the rest of the lease term. Before signing the lease, make sure you know exactly how long you're obligated to pay rent and the possible penalties you could incur.

656. If you live in an apartment, you may want to prepay an entire semester's worth of rent when you receive your financial aid disbursement, especially if you have trouble managing your funds and making them last for the whole semester. This way you won't be tempted to spend that money on something else and end up having to borrow to cover the rent. Get a written receipt whenever you make rent payments.

657. If you share an apartment, and the lease or any of the utilities are in your name, make sure your roommates pay their share promptly. You're the one ultimately responsible for the entire bill, and if payments are late, it will affect your credit history and your ability to get apartments and utilities in your name in the future.

Save Money on Food

658. When you buy a meal plan, you pay for all the meals whether you eat them or not, so sign up for fewer rather than more meals. For example, most students find they're not out and about in time to eat breakfast in the cafeteria, so a meal plan with two meals a day may be more than enough. If, after your first semester, you find you eat out or fix something in your dorm room fairly often, you may want to buy a meal plan for only one meal a day.

659. Buy coffee at the grocery store and make it at home. A daily Starbucks or other gourmet coffee can cost $3 or $4 a day, $28 a week, $112 per month, $448 a semester, or $996 per school year—and that's nearly $4,000 during a four-year degree program. Save the gourmet coffee for special occasions or the occasional treat instead of making it a daily habit.

660. Don't go grocery shopping when you're hungry. Studies have shown that you're much more likely to buy more than you need if you shop on an empty stomach. The best time to go shopping for food is after you've just eaten.

661. The best way to save on groceries is to plan ahead. Figure out the main meals for the week plus your favorite snacks and staples, like milk, eggs, and bread. Shop with a list; then stick to it, and you'll save money. Anything not on the list is an impulse purchase that should be avoided.

662. If you live in an apartment, get four to six friends together, pool your grocery money for your evening meals, and take turns cooking. It costs less per person, you'll eat better, you get to try other people's cooking, and you'll enjoy socializing.

663. Collect coupons for grocery and household items you normally buy. You can shave significant amounts off your grocery bill as long as you don't buy something you wouldn't normally buy just because you have a coupon for it. Your local Sunday newspaper usually includes a pack of coupons, and you can ask family members to save them for you, too.

664. Two words: ramen noodles. Sure, they're a cliché in college, but they actually have a place in your meal plan. How can you beat three meals for a dollar? For a more substantial meal, try bulking it up by throwing in steamed veggies and pieces of leftover chicken, another meat, or tofu.

665. Find out if there's a local food co-op in your college town. You can save a lot of money by buying items like dry beans, pasta, rice, oatmeal, peanut butter, herbs and spices, and other dry goods in bulk, without the expensive packaging found in grocery stores.

666. Make a list of the items you purchase on a regular basis (toiletries, paper products, cleaning supplies, certain foods) and compare prices at three different stores. Do your regular shopping at the store that offers lower prices on the items you buy most frequently.

667. Limit your grocery shopping to one or two stores. The price of gas for driving around town chasing a few pennies here and there will quickly eat into any savings. Also, every time you enter another grocery store the likelihood of making an impulse purchase goes up.

668. Pack your own lunch when you know you'll be on campus all day. Packed lunches are cheaper than buying food at the cafeteria or from vending machines, and you can eat them anywhere.

669. If your parents or other family members want to send you a care package, encourage them to send you nonperishable food (boxed macaroni and cheese, rice mixes, canned goods, cereal, and snack foods) to help reduce your grocery bills.

670. Avoid buying food or beverages at gourmet specialty shops and convenience markets. These stores are always more expensive than a grocery store.

671. The larger the supermarket, the better the prices overall. To minimize your grocery costs, do most of your shopping at the largest grocery store near you.

672. Learn to recognize the sales techniques used in grocery stores to encourage you to spend more money. For example, the most expensive products are usually placed at eye level so you notice them first. Look up and down to save money. Impulse items, like candy bars, cold sodas, and magazines, are placed at the ends of the aisles and at the checkout stands.

673. Don't pay for two meals and eat only one. That's what you're doing when you buy a meal plan for a set number of meals and you eat out instead of eating all the meals you already paid for.

674. Before using a coupon on a name brand item, do the math to see if generic brand item you usually buy is still cheaper. If so, the coupon actually costs you money.

675. When grocery shopping, remember that convenience comes at a cost. Laborsaving products, like shredded cheese, peeled carrots, and precut lettuce or salads cost more. Do the work yourself and save money.

676. Avoid buying foods that aren't in season in your part of the country. Fresh strawberries in Minnesota in January are going to cost more than you should spend. Buy fruit and vegetables when they're in season and you'll save money.

677. Brand-name foods are not necessarily any better than generic brands. In fact, brand-name companies often manufacture the generic brand foods that are sold under a store name or other off-brand-name. These items are cheaper because they don't come with the huge advertising costs that brand-name companies incur to sell their products.

678. Having a mini-fridge and a microwave in your dorm room can save you money that you might otherwise spend on take-out or fast-food. If you don't feel like hiking over to the cafeteria but you need sustenance, it's nice to be able to throw something together, like boxed macaroni and cheese, soup, boxed mashed potatoes, nachos and cheese, cereal, and so on.

679. Before going out to a restaurant or bar, plan how much you can afford to pay and then stick to that amount. If you don't plan ahead, you're much more likely to overspend and end up regretting it later when you're struggling to make ends meet.

680. Buy pasta in the bulk aisle of the grocery store. It's cheap and filling and can be prepared in limitless ways, plus it's easily stored. Look up recipes on the Internet.

681. In addition to comparing prices between stores, compare prices between brands. Most grocery chains have their own line of grocery items that are almost always cheaper than those of the large national food manufacturers. For example, IGAs often carry the Shur Fine line.

682. Limit your grocery store purchases to groceries. For non-grocery items, like paper towels, bathroom tissue, and cleaning supplies, shop at a larger chain retailer like Sam's Club or Costco. The prices will be lower, especially if you buy in bulk.

683. Plan ahead so you can limit your trips to the grocery store to one per week. The less often you go, the less likely you are to buy things on impulse and the less you'll spend on groceries.

684. Relying on fast food, convenience food, and frozen dinners not only adds pounds and drains your energy, but it also drains your wallet. You get more bang from your buck if you buy fresh fruits and vegetables and lean meats and cook them yourself. If you're clueless in the kitchen, read a book like *The College Student's Guide to Eating Well On Campus* by Ann Selkowitz Litt, or ask your Mom to show you a few simple dishes.

685. Get a bunch of friends or dormmates together on weekends and have a potluck dinner or assign items (salad, dessert, casserole) to save money. It's cheaper than eating out and is a great way to socialize.

686. Stop by your local fast-food place at closing time and ask if they have any food they're going to get rid of that didn't sell. Some managers would rather see the food go to college students than get thrown away, so you may score some pizza, sandwiches, or other grub.

687. Check out which restaurants offer free appetizers (usually during happy hour) and hang out for a while. Restaurants hope customers will drink enough alcohol, which has a very high mark-up, to make up for the cost of the free food. Buy a glass of soda for $1.50 and you may get to eat $5 or more worth of food.

688. Buy your food, household products, and supplies at off-campus stores. You'll pay less.

689. Avoid buying single serving sizes of snacks. You'll pay more for smaller servings because of the added cost of packaging. Buy larger sizes and break them down into baggies containing a serving size.

690. Keep a refillable water bottle and light snacks like apples, raisins, and nuts, in your backpack so you're not tempted by the vending machines on campus, where prices are marked up. Fill your water bottle at the fountains in the buildings on campus.

691. Call around to a number of pizza places and sandwich shops that you like to eat at or get carryout from and ask if they have weekly specials. Try to plan the days you eat out around the times when your favorite places offer their specials so you can lower your food costs.

Reduce the Cost of Utilities

692. If you live in an apartment and pay utilities, cut costs by conserving electricity. Turn off lights when not in use.

693. If you pay your own water bills, conserve water by avoiding long showers and doing full loads of laundry. In many towns, there's a separate charge for sewer service, and you're charged for disposing of every gallon of water you use, in addition to the cost of the water itself.

694. Turn down the heat. If you're paying to heat your own living space, you can save dramatically by turning the thermostat back to sixty-five degrees during the day and sixty degrees at night. Wear sweaters or fleece shirts to stay warm, and cover up with a nice fleece throw while you're studying or watching television.

695. Turning your computer off when you're not using it can save $5 to $8 a month. If you live in an apartment where four of you have computers, you could save a total of $20 to $32 a month. That's nothing to sneeze at.

696. If you're paying for electricity, replace one-hundred-watt light bulbs with twenty-eight-watt compact fluorescents. They cost more to purchase, but save around $40 each in electricity costs over the life of the bulb.

Save Money on Your Telephone Bill

697. Long-distance services in the dorms are a moneymaking venture for your school, but can be a budget-busting venture for you because the rates are so high. Make your cell phone your only phone, shop around for the deal that best suits your calling habits (see www.letstalk.com), and avoid exceeding your free minutes.

698. Another alternative to college-provided long-distance services is www.net2phone.com or other Internet phone services. If your dorm has unlimited broadband Internet service, you can use your computer to make phone calls for as little as two cents per minute. For around $35 a month, you can make unlimited phone calls, keep your home area code, and save your parents money on their calls to you.

699. Find a free chat room where you and friends or family can "talk" online. You'll avoid long-distance telephone charges, which are one of the largest expenses for most college students.

700. Use email or instant messaging instead of calling long-distance to keep in touch with friends and family. Save the phone for special occasions. When you do call long-distance, do so during off-peak hours to reduce the costs.

701. If you have landline phone service at school, get only the basics. Services like call waiting, caller ID, and three-way calling add unnecessary costs that add up over the course of the school year.

702. If you keep your cell phone calling plan when you go away to college, you'll incur roaming fees unless you have a plan that covers a wide geographic area and treats all calls in that area as local calls. Before you use your cell phone at college, call your provider and make sure you won't be incurring roaming fees. You may have to switch plans to a local provider.

703. Directory assistance is the lazy person's way of looking up a phone number, and can cost you between $.60 and $1.10 each time you use the service. Look up numbers in the phone book or online at www.anywho.com or www.switchboard.com, where the information is free. Even worse is the fee to have your phone ring when a busy number you tried to call becomes available. Fees like these, although seemingly inconsequential, are a waste of money and can add up over the course of a month or a semester.

704. Avoid making collect or third-party telephone calls. They're an expensive way to phone home.

705. Keep a calling card handy for situations where you can't make a call directly. You won't always be able to rely on your cell phone.

706. Consider asking your parents to get a toll-free number so you can call home whenever you want to. No extra phone line is needed.

707. Make international calls using a pre-paid phone card. International calls from your dorm or college-provided phone system will be prohibitively expensive.

708. Stay away from calling card plans that use your credit card. It's much too easy to overspend and you'll end up paying interest on top of the cost of the call if you can't pay your credit card balance in full at the end of the month. You'll also tie up your available credit, which you may need for something more important.

709. If you switch cell phone plans, watch out for the termination fee. Most companies charge nearly $200 if you terminate your plan in less than two years, unless you sign up for a bigger and better (more expensive) plan. Get all the facts before you make a move.

710. Don't dial 900 numbers or other telephone numbers that involve a fee for a service like news, sports, weather, traffic, or the time. You can get this information free in other places, including the Internet, newspapers, radio, and TV.

711. Before buying a cell phone, make sure the carrier has service in the area where you'll be attending school. You wouldn't be happy to commit to a two-year plan with a $175 early termination fee only to find when you got to school that your carrier doesn't operate in that area. You'd be stuck with the cost of signing up for a duplicate plan (with duplicate costs) or incurring the dreaded, and wasteful, early termination fee. It's best to wait until you get to campus to buy a cell phone.

712. Don't buy cell phone insurance. It's a waste of money.

713. Plan ahead so you can make long-distance telephone calls during off-peak hours, when the rates are lowest. This is usually in the evening or on weekends.

714. Before choosing a cell phone plan or a long-distance calling plan, ask yourself these questions: How many minutes will I be talking on the phone each month? What time of day do I make the bulk of my calls? Where do I call? Consider your answers to these questions when choosing your plan and you'll save money by getting the plan that fits your calling patterns.

715. If you'd like a cell phone only for emergencies, any cell phone will do, without paying for a calling plan. All cell phones will work for 911 calls anywhere you can receive a signal. You don't have to pay a cent. Find a used cell phone at a yard sale or talk to friends who are planning to buy a new cell phone and ask for their old one.

716. Long-distance telephone costs can be a bone of contention among roommates when sharing a dorm room or apartment if it's unclear who is responsible for the cost of some of the calls when the bill arrives. Keeping a log near the phone where everyone records the date, time, and place of their long-distance calls can prevent you from getting stuck paying for calls you didn't make.

717. If a simple log doesn't do the trick to prevent confusion about which roommate made which long-distance calls, take advantage of the managed long-distance services provided by many telephone companies. You can block all toll calls from your landline by contacting your service provider, or you can elect to require a PIN number in order to place a long-distance call. Other options may also be available.

Save Money on Clothing and Laundry

718. Don't buy clothes that require dry cleaning. They're expensive to maintain and cost money every time you wear them. If you buy a skirt on sale for $25 but it requires dry cleaning, you'll have doubled your cost after cleaning it five times (assuming the average $5 dry cleaning charge for skirts). Stick to clothing that is easy and inexpensive to care for.

719. Do full loads of laundry. Those quarters you feed the washers and dryers add up, not to mention the cost of detergent and fabric softener. Also, clothes dry faster when there's a full load in the dryer.

720. If you pay for your own utilities, use cold water for washing clothes whenever possible, and always rinse in cold water. You'll save money by avoiding the cost of heating hot water.

721. Always set a timer so you can add fabric softener to the laundry cycle at the appropriate time. Adding softener at the end and then putting the load through an additional rinse cycle adds up to significant additional costs if you're paying for your own water, because it takes approximately ten gallons of water for the typical rinse cycle.

722. Cut fabric softener sheets in half. You won't even notice the difference in the results, and a box will last twice as long.

723. Frequent washing wears out clothing. If you wear a piece of clothing gently, you shouldn't have to wash it every time you wear it. Hang it up when you take it off. If you throw it in a heap of dirty clothes on the floor, you'll have to wash it whether it needs it or not.

724. If your parents' home is close enough to college to go home once or twice a month, take your laundry with you. You can save $2.00 per load to wash, and $1.05 per load to dry at $.35 per ten minutes, plus soap, bleach, and fabric softener, for an average of $3.50 per load). At three loads per week, that's a savings of $10.50 per week, $42 per month or $168 per semester.

725. Love your laundry. Proper care of your clothing will make it last longer while still looking good. Taking care of your clothing according to the fabric and the care instructions on each item will reduce the cost of your wardrobe.

726. You know that throwing a wool sweater into the dryer will reduce it to Barbie doll size, but did you know that washing rayon in hot water could do just as much damage? Know your fabrics, and launder accordingly. Hand-wash delicate fabrics and hang them to air-dry.

727. Invest a few bucks in a couple of good-quality stain removers—one for wash-ables and one for dry cleanables. As soon as you spill something on a piece of clothing, treat it with the appropriate stain remover and launder it. Stains that are allowed to set may never come out and you'll have to toss the item or use it for doing housework.

728. Buy a box of stain remover towelettes, like Shout, in individual packages and tuck a few in your purse, your car, and your backpack so you can treat stains promptly no matter where you are.

729. Zipper not working? Instead of throwing the garment out and buying a new one or relegating it to the back of your closet, rub the stubborn zipper with a bit of bar soap or paraffin and soon you'll be slip-sliding away.

730. Turn your clothing inside out before you throw it in the washer. It helps prevent abrasions on dark fabrics and will reduce annoying and unsightly pilling of knit fabrics.

731. Whenever possible, hang your clothes to dry instead of throwing them in the dryer. They'll last longer. Heat is hard on fabrics, especially knits or anything with spandex or elastic. If you must use the dryer, use the lowest heat setting possible.

732. Sort your clothes before washing. Separate dark, white, and light colored clothing into separate loads to prevent ruining clothes when colors bleed from one fabric onto another. This is especially true when you are washing new, dark clothes. New clothes will surely bleed during the first wash.

733. If the color from one piece of clothing bleeds onto another, use color remover sheets (available at your grocery or discount store in the detergent section) to remove the extra color. Do it as soon as possible for best results.

734. Don't leave your laundry unattended in the laundry room. You may find yourself having to fork out some hard-earned cash to replenish your wardrobe. Dorms are notorious for disappearing clothing left unattended in the washers or dryers.

735. When planning your school wardrobe, buy items that coordinate and mix and match so that one item (blouse, sweater, or jacket, for instance) can be used with several different outfits. It will make your wardrobe appear larger and you won't get as bored with your clothes and feel the need to buy more.

736. Plan your wardrobe. Don't buy clothes on impulse. Ask yourself: Do I need this? Do I really want it? Will I still want it tomorrow or next week or next month? Can I live without it? If not, can I buy it later (maybe for less)? Will it be on sale soon, or could I buy it somewhere else for less? Does it go with other clothes I already own so I can make more outfits by mixing and matching? Does it fit my lifestyle? If you answer these questions before you plunk down the cash, you won't have clothes hanging in your closet that you never wear or that you paid so much for that you feel you have to save for special occasions.

737. Buy clothes at the end of the season, not before or during the season. Summer clothes are usually cheapest in August and September, winter clothes in March and April. Back-to-school sales usually take place from mid-August to mid-September. Plan your shopping accordingly.

738. Always pay cash for clothes. Clothing is one of the categories that college students overspend most on, and paying with a credit card encourages overspending. Using cash will help you stay within your budget.

739. When shopping for clothes, go directly to the clearance rack. If there's nothing there you absolutely love or really need, leave empty-handed and come back another time. In addition to saving you money, bargain hunting can be fun.

740. Buy good quality shoes at a reasonable price. When the heels or soles begin to wear, take them to a shoe repair shop. You'll get more mileage for your money than you would if you bought cheaper shoes more frequently.

741. Match your clothing to your activity. Don't wear your best jeans to do yard work. Don't clean the bathroom in your cashmere sweater or silk blouse. Don't hike in the woods in your expensive shoes. Dress appropriately for your activity and you'll save money by making your clothes last longer.

742. Don't buy a new wardrobe for your first semester away at college. The weather may be totally different than it is at home, and you'll make better decisions once you see what everyone else is wearing and know what you feel comfortable in. Set aside some money to purchase a few new items once you've accessed weather, local styles, and your college atmosphere.

743. Understand how auto insurance is calculated so you can make decisions that will reduce your premiums. The cost of your auto insurance is based on factors such as your age and driving record; the age, repair record, and cost of the make and model of the car you drive; your credit history; the distance between school and home; and your grades. Some of these things you have no control over, but you can reduce your costs by maximizing the things you can control that affect your rates.

744. If you attend school at least 100 miles from home and you don't take your car with you, make sure you or your parents inform the insurance company. The premiums should go down substantially while you're not using the car on a regular basis.

745. If you own a car, don't ever go without auto insurance. You risk your financial future. Without insurance, you could be sued and forced into bankruptcy, ruining your credit for many years. Even if you drive an old clunker and decide it's not worth covering for collision damage, make sure it's covered for liability.

746. If you belong to a fraternity or sorority, an honor society, or other student organization, let your auto insurance company know. Some insurers offer discounts to members of various clubs and other organizations.

747. Your auto insurance will be dramatically cheaper if you can stay on your parents' policy while in college. Once you're listed as the primary driver on a vehicle, you're considered a higher risk and your premium costs will probably double. Whenever possible, stay on your parents' policy as a secondary driver so you can benefit from the price break that their age provides. Your parents will also receive a discount for having a multi-car policy.

748. If you take a car to school, make sure you notify the insurance company of where the car will be located. If you don't, they may not cover claims for theft or damage.

749. You can save money by getting on the Dean's List. Ask your insurance company if they offer a "good student" discount on auto insurance.

750. Ask your parents to call their insurance agent to make sure your stuff will be covered while you're at school, especially any computer or electronic equipment you take with you. These items are often targets of thieves and are easily stolen (especially laptop computers and other electronic equipment).

751. Don't buy insurance you don't need. This includes credit insurance, the collision damage waiver on car rentals (check to make sure your auto insurance includes this coverage), flight insurance, and extended warranties.

752. Don't fall for sales pitches for credit card loss protection insurance. The law already protects you from fraudulent use of your credit card if it's lost or stolen. Buying this "insurance" is throwing away your money.

753. Don't "go bare" (we're not talking about skinny dipping here). Going bare means not being covered by insurance—in this case, health insurance. If you have a serious illness or accident, it could wipe out not only your own finances, but also your family's if they have to pay your medical bills.

754. If at all possible, stay on your parents' health insurance policy through graduation from college. Most policies allow dependent students enrolled full-time (at least twelve credits per semester) at an accredited college to be covered under their parents' policy until the age of twenty-three. You may have to show proof of enrollment as a full-time student once a year.

755. If your parents' health insurance coverage is a managed care program, like an HMO, which requires you to use medical providers in a local network, you may not be able to benefit from their plan. It will make sense to continue your coverage only if your college is close enough to your parents' home to enable you to return there when you need medical care.

756. If you can't continue to be covered under your parents' health insurance policy, check into the school's health insurance programs. The coverage may not be great, but it's usually relatively inexpensive, and you should never be without any coverage at all. Being young and healthy doesn't guarantee you won't need medical care, and uninsured medical costs can force you into bankruptcy.

757. If you're in a fraternity or sorority, you may be eligible for group health insurance coverage provided by your national chapter at a reasonable rate. Contact the national headquarters for details.

758. When you borrow money for a car or other large purchase, or sign up for a credit card, you may be offered a payment protection plan, or credit insurance, which claims to cover your payments if you become disabled or unemployed. Most of these plans actually pay only your minimum payment, which isn't enough to pay down your balance and barely covers your interest costs. These plans are just another moneymaking tool for credit card companies and a waste of your money.

12.

Having Fun without a Lot of Dough

The college lifestyle is unlike any other you'll ever experience, yet in addition to the unique financial challenges faced by students, there are many that are common to adults everywhere. The availability of student loan money has made the lifestyle of today's students much different than it ever was in the past, with some students living the high life and paying for it later with huge debts. There are many ways to significantly reduce the day-to-day costs of college in ways that seem small when considered individually but add up to tremendous sums over the course of four years. Some of these methods are relevant to anybody trying to save money and some are unique to students.

759. Limit booze, which is one of the most expensive habits of college students. If you get so wasted you can't remember the party, did you really get your money's worth? And is vomiting your idea of a good time? If you use alcohol in moderation you'll enjoy yourself more and it will cost you less.

760. Rather than purchasing new CDs on a regular basis, ask for your favorite CDs for birthdays, Christmas, or other gift-giving occasions, and swap CDs with your roommates or friends instead of buying new. One CD a week can cost you $60 a month or $720 a year—a lot for a college student to spend.

761. Don't use shopping as recreation, to get out of the dumps, or to cure boredom. Shop only when you have a specific item in mind that you really need. Window-shopping leads to impulse spending for items you didn't know you "needed" until you saw them in the store, and having to pay the bills later takes all the enjoyment out of it.

762. Find out who your roomies will be before the semester starts. Get in touch with them and plan who will bring what to school, so you don't waste money duplicating big-ticket items for your dorm room. Otherwise, you may end up with two mini-refrigerators and no microwave.

763. Avoid online gambling. It's addictive and your losses can add up quickly. Is it fair to your parents (and yourself) to blow the money they (and you) have worked so hard to come up with for your education?

764. While in college, live like a student, or you'll end up with so much debt you'll have to live like a student long after you graduate. Having more debt than you can handle after college is discouraging after working so hard to earn an education.

765. Small expenses can add up to big money. A cup of coffee at the local coffee shop before classes each morning can total $46 a month, or nearly $200 a semester. At $4.00 per pack, a pack-a-day smoking habit can total well over $500 per semester. It doesn't take too many of these and other small indulgences and incidentals to add up to thousands of dollars a semester. Pick one indulgence and forego the others, or cut back on them altogether.

766. Listen to your campus radio station for free tickets for movies, concerts, and other events. These stations are geared toward college students and have giveaways that are sure to be a hit.

767. Betting on football games or other sporting events can quickly deplete your cash and lead to a gambling addiction. The odds of winning are not worth the odds of losing, so if you're going to bet, do it for the fun and not the money; and limit yourself to a dollar or two. Avoid betting online altogether. It's even riskier and can be a sure recipe for disaster.

768. The most important financial lesson you can learn is to recognize the difference between your needs and your wants. At the beginning of the semester, make a list of each. Needs include true necessities, such as tuition, books, housing, food, and transportation. Wants are nearly everything else: CDs, DVDs, concerts, road trips, a big wardrobe, tattoos, body piercings, and happy hours. You don't have to deprive yourself of all your wants, but you should make thoughtful choices and remember that you have to make sacrifices in college so you can have a better life after graduation.

769. Check out garage sales, thrift or consignment shops, and eBay when looking for dorm furniture, decorations, and household items. People get rid of perfectly good stuff just because they don't need it anymore or have grown tired of it, and you can usually pick it up at a great price.

770. Often, you can find everything you need to equip your room from the people who are moving out of the dorm you are moving into. Upperclassmen may no longer need mini-fridges, carpeting, or lofts because they are moving into off-campus housing. Keep your eyes peeled for low-cost hand-me-downs.

771. Buy your supplies at discount office stores, not on campus, where they can cost up to several times more. Keep a supply of expendable supplies that you use regularly, like inkjet cartridges and copy paper, on hand so you always have a backup and won't be forced to buy on campus in an emergency.

772. Control the temptation to be a party animal in college. Strike a healthy balance between socializing and studying. By maintaining excellent grades, you'll continue to be eligible for additional scholarships and merit awards throughout your college years.

773. If you go to the movies regularly, ask about discount coupons. Movie theaters often sell booklets that include eight or ten tickets at a reduced price per ticket.

774. Learn to enjoy inexpensive entertainment and recreation. Use your imagination, not your wallet, to have fun.

775. You'd be surprised what interesting places you can discover within an hour or two of campus. Take day trips to surrounding areas and explore recreational areas, parks, zoos, beaches, hiking trails, historic landmarks, museums, and the like. Most of these things are free or very cheap, and provide an interesting date or outing with friends.

776. Go to a matinee movie and save almost half the price of an evening ticket. After the movie, you can spend the evening getting together with your friends at someone's house or dorm.

777. Have a weekly game night at your apartment or dorm. Ask everyone to bring their favorite board game and set up several tables with a different game at each table, then switch tables so everyone gets to socialize with everyone else. Listen to good music and have a few munchies for a fun evening.

778. Instead of going out to dinner, go out for dessert and coffee with friends. It's cheaper, and just as much fun.

779. Forego the goodies at the movie theater, where ten cents worth of popcorn can cost you five bucks, and sixteen ounces of cola can cost you the price of three or more two-liter bottles at the grocery store. Have a snack before you go so hunger won't tempt you to squander your money on overpriced candy, popcorn, and soda.

780. Instead of paying top dollar to see a first-run movie in the theater, invite a bunch of friends over for the evening and watch a movie on Pay-Per-View. Throw in some munchies and drinks, and you can all chip in on the cost for lots less than you would have paid at the theater.

781. Don't date your way into debt. Consider it a challenge to come up with ideas for inexpensive dates. Often creative outings that cost little or no money make the most memorable dating experiences and a better impression on your date.

782. Students in a number of colleges have been targeted for lawsuits by the music industry for downloading and swapping music illegally. Avoid the temptation to use peer-to-peer music services like Kazaa and Grokster, which besides being illegal, are laced with pop-up ads, spyware, and viruses that put your computer and personal financial information at risk.

783. If you and your friends rent lots of movies, instead of renting DVDs from your local rental store, sign up at Netflix.com. For $20 a month you can order an unlimited number of rental DVDs, receive them in the mail, and keep them for as long as you want to. When you're ready, stick them in the mail and return them postage free.

784. Your local Blockbuster movie store may offer a program similar to the one offered by Netflix. Check it out and compare benefits and costs.

785. Drop HBO from your cable TV lineup and save $144 or more per year. Most movies can be seen on network television within a few months of appearing on HBO.

786. Wait for movies to hit the discount movie theaters. By waiting a couple of months, you'll save $6 or more per movie. This adds up over the course of the year, especially if you go to the movies often.

787. Instead of buying TV Guide, you can also look up local TV schedules on the Internet at www.tvguide.com. You can also get the same information in the Sunday paper, in free papers distributed locally in your neighborhood, or at the grocery store.

788. Make your social life revolve primarily around campus events, which are often either free or very cheap. Sporting events, movies, plays, concerts, bowling, dances, game nights, and more take place every week on most campuses, and the price is unbeatable.

789. If there's a magazine you absolutely must have, don't buy it on the newsstands or at the grocery store. Buy a subscription and save up to 80 percent off the newsstand price. Better yet, ask for a subscription from your parents or other family member as a gift.

790. Kill two birds with one stone by taking part in activities on campus. Not only are many fun campus activities free, they often include free food, so you can reduce your grocery costs while having a good time.

791. Look into the best sites online where you can listen and buy music on demand. At Napster's new site (www.napster.com), you can listen to and download an unlimited amount of music for a monthly fee. You can keep the music on your computer or MP3 player, and also hook up the MP3 player to your car.

792. Also look into Rhapsody (www.rhapsody.com), where you pay an inexpensive monthly fee to listen to as much music as you want. When you know that you like a song and want to download it, you can download individual songs for a small fee. Use a site like this to curb the urge to buy overpriced CDs from a music store, especially when you may only like a few tracks on an album.

Prepare for the Cost of Greek Life

793. At most colleges, fraternities and sororities are rarely like their depiction in the movie Animal House, although some do have a reputation for partying. The so-called Greek Life or Greek system dominates the social scene at some schools, and a large number of students join up. Greek Life has many benefits, but it's not cheap, so before you decide on whether it's for you, talk to members of the sorority or fraternity you're interested in and ask about the costs.

794. Room and board in a sorority or fraternity house is usually similar to dorm costs, but if you're thinking of participating in Greek Life, be prepared for fees over and above the cost of living in the house. Initiation fees for pledges can total several hundred dollars, and other fees can add up to several thousand dollars a year.

795. Ask about the average semester fees for the sororities or fraternities you plan to rush, and make sure there's enough room in your budget. Be prepared to pay more for the first semester of Greek Life, because of the initiation fee, which is typically between $90 and $200. You'll also have to buy special clothing to identify you as a pledge, and you'll be required to participate in activities that will cost money.

796. National and local sorority or fraternity dues run between $425 and $800 per semester at most colleges. If you can't swing this additional cost, you may be able to obtain financial assistance from the organization.

797. Some sororities and fraternities include meals for an additional fee of around $300 per semester for five meals a week. Do the math. It could be a really good deal per meal.

798. When making plans for spring break travel, keep in mind that some deals are too good to be true. Unscrupulous travel companies target students, because students like to travel and they don't always do their homework when buying travel services. Being the victim of a travel scam can be a serious financial setback, so check out the travel company thoroughly to make sure they're legit, get everything in writing, and read all the fine print.

799. If you're driving somewhere for the weekend or for a school break, let people know you'd be interested in sharing the ride. If several people chip in to cover the costs of gas, you'll all save money. Campuses usually have a common ride board where you can post your destination.

800. Make sure all details you've been told verbally are in writing, including the trip cancellation policy and what items are included free, such as meals. Don't assume anything, and don't count on anything that's not documented.

801. For those trips back home for the holidays or summer breaks, save money on airfare by comparing prices on an airfare search engine like www.sidestep.com or www.orbitz.com. To get the best deals, check back often for price updates.

802. Look for hidden fees on deals that claim to cover all your travel expenses. For example, many cruises that include "all fees" charge passengers when they dock in a foreign port. These types of hidden fees can add up enough to blow your budget.

803. Check out the travel company you use to make your spring break travel arrangements before you pay any money down. Call your local Better Business Bureau or use their website at www.bbb.org to check for complaints against the company.

804. To get decent rates on spring break travel, plan well in advance, especially if you're going to a hot spot like a tropical island during the peak season. Airlines typically set aside only a few seats on each flight at discounted rates, so if you don't book early, you may end up sitting next to someone who paid $150 for their seat and wondering why you paid $400 for yours.

805. Take advantage of airfare search engines to find the best prices on airfare for spring break and other travel. Besides services like Orbitz.com, CheapTickets.com, Travelocity.com, QIXO.com, CheapFares.com, Hotwire.com, and Expedia.com, there are those that cater only to students, such as Student Universe (www.studentuniverse.com), STA Travel (www.statravel.com), Student Traveler (www.studenttraveler.com), and Travelosophy (www.itravelosophy.com).

806. Before you enter a foreign country, make sure you know the laws that might affect you, like what substances are illegal, what the legal drinking age is, and so on. You don't want to be thrown into a Mexican prison, for example, and left there without any notification to family or friends.

807. Plan your trips back home well in advance so you can take advantage of the best available airfares. The best rates often require 21-, 14-, or 7-day advance booking, and they sell out fast.

808. Travel on off-peak days. Airfares are generally more expensive on Mondays and Fridays due to business travel on those days. Your best days for cheaper travel are Tuesday through Thursday and Friday night through Sunday morning. Plan accordingly to save money.

809. For cheaper airfares, plan to stay over a Saturday night. You'll save up to two-thirds off the standard price.

810. You can save money by booking flights last minute, but only do so when you're flexible about the travel days, because there's no guarantee you'll get a flight on a particular day. Check the airlines' websites regularly for notices of discounted last-minute fares, or use www.webflyer.com's "Deal Watch" feature.

811. It's cheaper to take a train than fly, and sometimes just as fast when all the shouting is over. Amtrak trains offer student discounts. Search your options online on the Amtrak website at www.amtrak.com.

812. Buses seem slow compared to flying, but when you factor in travel time to and from the airport, arriving two hours early for security check-in, stopovers in other cities, and possible delays, you may get there just as fast by bus if you're not traveling great distances. Greyhound offers discounts to students on many of its bus routes. Check them out at www.greyhound.com/student/index.asp.

813. Nonstop flights are sometimes more expensive than those with one stop on the way. Check out all the options for getting to your destination. A little flexibility could save you a lot of money.

814. Once you purchase an airline ticket, don't expect to get a refund if you change your mind. You can usually change the ticket for a different day or flight on the same airline for an administrative fee, usually around $100.

815. If you have to go home unexpectedly because of a death or serious illness in your family, ask the airline about their bereavement fares. You'll have to answer some detailed questions and may have to produce documentation, but you'll probably get a substantial discount.

816. Airlines routinely overbook flights to compensate for no-shows, and sometimes they have to ask for volunteers to take a different flight. They generally offer a financial incentive, like a free ticket or $100 off the price of an airfare. Let the stewardess know when you board that you'd be willing to be bumped if needed.

817. Fly or ride standby. Instead of having a guaranteed seat on the plane, train, or bus, you'll only get on if there's an available seat after all the people with reservations have been seated. Your ticket will be cheaper.

818. If you know you'll be using the train or bus regularly for trips home, buy a pass good for multiple trips. They usually have a lower cost per trip.

819. Opt for electronic airline tickets. There's nothing worse than getting stuck in an airport on Christmas Eve because you've lost your ticket. E-tickets give you peace of mind and prevent you from having to purchase a new ticket if you lose yours.

820. Sign up with airlines that service your hometown area to receive their email alerts about cheap tickets for unbooked seats. These tickets are usually available a few days before the flight at a steeply reduced price.

821. The worst time to travel is between Thanksgiving and Christmas. Expect to pay more and encounter more hassles and delays. Seats during these times book early; so don't rely on last-minute deals if you want to get home for the holidays.

822. Be flexible about your flight times. Sure, it would be nice to depart and arrive in the daylight when you're bright-eyed and bushy-tailed. They don't call a middle-of-the-night flight the "red-eye" for nothing, but you can save a significant amount of money by taking less popular flights (late at night or in the wee hours of the morning).

823. If your destination is within a couple of hours of several major airports, check the cost of flights to each one. You may find that a two-hour drive to get to a different airport will save you $100 or more.

824. Avoid purchasing airline tickets on weekends. Airlines update prices three times a day during the week and once a day on weekends in order to maximize their profits by filling flights. It's better for them to offer you a cheap seat when it looks like a flight won't fill than to have the plane fly with the seat empty. You'll have the best chance of getting a cheap flight if you buy right after an update.

825. When making travel arrangements, ask if your deposit is refundable. Don't settle for the salesperson's word—get it in writing.

826. Don't settle for vague descriptions like "major hotels" or "major airlines" when booking travel arrangements, especially to places outside the U.S. You may find yourself flying on a four-seat prop plane full of chickens and staying in a large tent on the beach. Get names, addresses, and phone numbers of all travel providers such as airlines and hotels, and call them to verify the details of your reservations.

827. If you're told that you've won a free vacation, ask if you have to buy something else in order to get it. Some scams offer "free" airfare but require you to buy expensive hotel accommodations. It ends up costing you more than it would have if you'd paid normal airfare and made your own lodging arrangements.

828. If your baggage is lost or damaged during your flight, the airline should reimburse you in some manner. Report the loss or damage to the baggage claim office. Insist on a form that you fill out and file with the airline before you leave the airport.

829. Make sure airfares are quoted with the return fare included. Many operators quote the one-way fare, hoping you won't notice the fine print. Also make sure the hotel that's included actually exists or you may find out that when they said you'd be staying at "The Dunes," you'd actually be camping out on the beach.

830. Anytime you make a deposit, whether it's a security deposit for an apartment or a deposit for a trip, there's a chance you won't get it back. Make sure you get all the stipulations surrounding the return of your deposit in writing, and get a written receipt.

831. College bowl games are fun and a popular outing for students, but they can be expensive. Limit your bowl trips to those in the immediate area where you attend school unless you can combine the game with a trip home or somewhere you need to go for other reasons. Most students use credit cards to pay for travel to bowl games, and because they don't have the money to pay the balance off quickly, they incur high interest costs on top of the trip expenses.

Nine Tips for Avoiding Parking Tickets

832. The best way to avoid parking tickets is to avoid driving a car on campus. Walk or bike instead. Your body and your wallet will thank you for it.

833. Parking is big business in college towns. For instance, fines for parking violations at the University of Colorado at Boulder totaled nearly $1.25 million last year. This is money students can ill-afford to throw away. Know your campus parking regulations inside and out and make a concerted effort to follow them.

834. Be careful where you park in town near campus. Because parking is so often in short supply on campus, students who can't find on-campus parking try to park as close to campus as possible. Local police patrol these areas looking for parking violators. Many cities collect millions of dollars a year in student parking fines, in addition to the fines collected by the school for on-campus violations.

835. Don't park in handicapped parking spaces on campus unless you have a handicapped sticker. At $50 to $300 per occurrence, it's one of the most costly parking mistakes you can make.

836. If you hate to clock-watch, avoid metered parking spaces on campus. Some of the places you'll most likely want to park have short turnover times because they're high traffic spots (like the bookstore). If your meter runs out you could get a $15 ticket or worse.

837. The parking violations that typically carry the greatest fines are parking in a handicapped space without a valid handicapped permit, parking in the fire lane, blocking traffic, and displaying a lost, stolen, or counterfeit parking permit. If you feel forced to park in a spot you know may earn you a ticket, at least try to avoid these particular infractions.

838. If you park in the tow-away loading zone in back of campus buildings or your dorm, your chances of getting slapped with a fine are high. It's better to park farther away and walk.

839. It's bad enough to get a $15 parking ticket, but if your car is towed because of a parking violation, you could pay up to $100 in towing costs. To avoid an expensive fine, allow plenty of time when going somewhere in order to increase your chances of finding a legal parking spot.

840. If your car does get towed, make sure to retrieve it the same day. Otherwise, you'll pay not only the towing fee and parking ticket, but also an additional $25 or more per day for storage until you retrieve your car and pay your balance.

Cut Transportation Costs

841. Some colleges have free shuttle service on campus to help you get around easily and quickly. If yours offers this service, there's no sense in bringing a car onto campus, where you'll probably have trouble finding parking and may end up getting a parking ticket. Take advantage of the shuttle service instead.

842. If you're in the market for a car, buy used. You can get a like-new two- or three-year-old car for nearly half the price of new because cars depreciate in value so quickly the first few years.

843. Resist the urge to use your limited funds to add cool additions to your car while you're in college, like raising or lowering it, adding decals or a spoiler, getting a custom paint job, or installing a fancy CD player or stereo system. You'll end up borrowing to cover other expenses. Wait until you're out of school and have more expendable income.

844. Gasoline expands in the heat. If you buy during the cool part of the day, when gas is less dense, you'll get a little more for your money. Also know it doesn't make sense to "top off" your gas tank. When gas expands in the heat, you'll lose some down the overflow tube. Besides, those short bursts on the pump handle run up the meter but don't really deliver much gas to your tank.

845. Don't buy premium gasoline. It's considerably more expensive and only cars with high-performance engines require it. That doesn't include your Honda Civic or your VW Bug. Like most cars, they're perfectly happy with regular.

846. Check the pressure in your tires every week. Every pound of underinflation costs you 6 percent in gas efficiency. If you normally pay $60 a month for gas, and you're riding around on tires that should have pressure of 32 psi but only have 29 psi, you'll end up paying an extra $11 a month in gas.

847. College students can be sitting ducks when it comes to auto repairs. Repairs can be expensive and the auto repair industry has more than its share of rip-offs. Check around in your college town for a reputable repair shop and ask locals for recommendations before you need work done. You'll be able to act quickly when you have a problem, without the stress of finding a mechanic on short notice, and you'll reduce your chances of getting ripped-off.

848. Check your oil often and have it changed every 3,000 to 4,000 miles. It's the number one way to extend the life of your car's engine and help avoid costly repairs. If you're handy, you can do it yourself. Just be sure to use the type and weight of oil recommended by the manufacturer.

849. Learn a little about cars so you can spot small problems before they turn into big, expensive problems. Learn what looks like trouble, sounds like trouble, smells like trouble, and feels like trouble, and act promptly when these symptoms appear.

850. Stay within the speed limit. Speeding tickets are expensive in more ways than one. You'll not only get slapped with a substantial fine, you'll have a speeding ticket on your driving record, which will raise your car insurance premiums.

851. If you have a car at school, transportation may be one of your biggest expenses after tuition and room and board. Drive a gas-efficient car, not a gas-guzzler like an SUV, and keep your driving record clean to keep your insurance costs down.

852. If you're planning to rent a truck to haul your stuff to college, consider U-Haul's free online bulletin board that helps you hook up with other students headed in the same direction. By sharing a truck and taking turns driving, you can save money and make the trip more enjoyable.

853. If you rent a truck to move your belongings to or from college, check with your insurance company to see if your auto policy will cover the truck. If not, be sure to sign up for the insurance offered by the truck rental company so you're protected from any liability.

854. If your car isn't covered on your parents' auto policy, shop around for auto insurance. You may be able to save hundreds of dollars a year by choosing one company over another, so get quotes from at least three.

855. Save big bucks by keeping a clean driving record. Auto insurance for anyone under twenty-five is very expensive (especially for men) and a speeding ticket or drinking violation can add thousands of dollars a year to your costs.

856. Contrary to what Detroit would have you believe, you aren't what you drive. Buy cars based on reliability, quality, safety, price, and cost to maintain, not on looks alone.

857. If you'll be buying a car to take to college, look beyond the purchase price or the monthly payment, and consider the cost of ownership. Does that model have a good repair record? Is it a gas hog? Will it cost more to insure? You might be able to afford to buy the car but not be able to afford to own it.

858. Gas has become a major expense for anybody who drives a car. Save money on gas by driving the speed limit, making smooth starts and stops, keeping your car tuned, and keeping your tires properly inflated.

859. If you buy a used car to take to college, check out its history by using an online service like www.carfax.com. Provide the car's vehicle identification number (VIN), usually found on a metal plate inside the windshield, and for a reasonable fee ($20 or so) you'll receive a history of the car's repair record. Stay away from cars that have been in serious accidents or floods, have a history of costly repairs, or have had their odometer tinkered with. Cars that were previously rental cars may not be the best choice (driven hard by many people), but leased cars are often good buys (taken care of because they have to be turned in at the end of the lease).

860. Warming up your car by letting it idle wastes nearly a quart of gas every 15 minutes and is a habit that can add up to a chunk of change over time. The engine actually warms up faster when driving than it does when idling.

861. You may be used to having a car at your disposal to get you around at home, but chances are you won't need one in college. Most campuses are compact and well laid-out, making a car unnecessary. You'll save a lot of headaches and a lot of money by leaving the car at home, at least for the first year or two.

862. Your auto insurance premiums are affected by your credit rating, so keep it squeaky clean. Pay bills on time, don't have too many credit cards, and don't max them out. You'll pay lower auto insurance premiums.

863. When buying a car, new or used, consider the total purchase price, not the monthly payments, which can look very attractive when stretched out over a longer period of time. Try to buy a car that you can pay off in three, or at the most, four years, or you could end up still making payments on a car that is worth less than you owe on it, which means you're stuck with it whether you still want it or not. You'll also pay much more interest.

864. If you decide you just can't do without your car at school, you'll save money on car insurance if you get good grades. Most major insurers offer a 25 percent discount to students under 25 who are on the Dean's List. Make sure your insurance agent knows you're a good student.

865. Leave your car at home and walk or bike whenever possible. You'll save money on gas, reduce wear and tear on your car, avoid parking tickets on campus, and keep off the infamous "freshman 15."

866. If you have a car at school, consider raising your deductible for collision coverage. If your car is more than eight years old, drop the collision coverage altogether and keep only the liability coverage. If you have an accident, your insurance will only pay the book value of the car, and after about six years, the book value on most cars is very low.

13.

Scout out Student Discounts

Never again in your life will you have the opportunities for getting discounts that you have while you're in college. Most college-town businesses cater to students, and there are a myriad of online discounts, discount membership cards, and discount booklets. Take full advantage of these opportunities to save money.

867. For $20 a year, you can get a Student Advantage card, which provides discounts of 10 to 50 percent at 15,000 locations. Purchase a card at a Greyhound bus terminal, pick up an order form at your campus bookstore or student union, or buy online at www.studentadvantage.com. Save on food, clothes, books, music, travel, toiletries, software, and more at any merchant that displays the "SA" logo; however, don't get sucked into buying things you didn't plan on just because you see discounts on them.

868. In addition to Student Advantage, look into other online student discount programs such as www.incard.com, and www.entertainment.com. You'll save money on entertainment, restaurants, travel, and more.

869. Your student ID card is your ticket to discounts on movies, museums, theaters, bars, restaurants, and other activities and products. Carry your card with you everywhere, and get in the habit of asking for a student discount even if you don't see a notice that discounts are offered.

870. Businesses in college towns cater to students by offering discounts on nearly everything. Browse local newspapers for coupons for food, toiletries, and other items you purchase regularly.

871. When planning to make a purchase, use an online price comparison search engine like www.pricegrabber.com, which lists merchants offering the item you're searching for at discounted prices. The difference in prices between stores is sometimes nothing short of amazing.

872. Going to the movies is a favorite student activity, and the costs can add up quickly (especially if you throw in popcorn and a soda). Find movie theaters that offer reduced prices, buy movie coupon books that offer discounts, attend cheaper matinees, or rent movies and watch them in your dorm.

873. Take advantage of the free or inexpensive activities that are available on most campuses. Get the college newspaper regularly, or find out where such activities are posted, and plan your social life around them.

874. Browse www.coolsavings.com and www.aroundcampus.com to look for coupons from local merchants for items you normally buy. When you find one you could use, print it out and carry it in your backpack so you'll have it with you when you need it.

875. You can't take advantage of the numerous discounts many businesses offer to students if you don't know about them. Ask your financial aid office if they have a list of local merchants' discounts.

876. When making any type of purchase, ask the merchant if they offer student discounts, even if you don't have a coupon and don't see a sign indicating that the business gives discounts to students.

877. Many online stores offer discounts if you have a coupon or promotion code, so a great way to get discounts on purchases is to enter the name of the product and store and the word "rebate" or "coupon" into the Google search engine at www.google.com. Once you find the coupon, enter the coupon code at checkout and voila! You have a discount. You can also find coupons to print out and use at brick and mortar stores.

878. As a college student, you may be eligible for heavy discounts on software. If you need database software, Web design software, Windows, Office, or other software for your course work, you may be able to get them for a fraction of the retail cost. Check online software sites that specialize in academic software or ask your instructor.

879. Take advantage of freebies online, and get free samples of everything imaginable. Make sure you use a reputable site like About.com's Freebies at freebies.about.com. Not only is it fun to get packages in the mail, you'll save money.

880. Many cultural organizations in college towns offer special prices to college students. Museums, symphonies, ballet, live theater, and concerts, are often heavily discounted if you have a student ID. The discounts make these activities great for dates and entertainment.

881. If you attend college in a town that has a public transportation system like a subway, ask about student discounts. Many transit authorities encourage students to use public transportation by offering significant discounts on monthly passes or other programs.

882. Since music meister Napster went legitimate, they've struck deals with some colleges to offer free or discounted legal digital music to students. Ask if your school has music on demand. If it's available, you won't feel compelled to purchase music.

14.

Get the Most Bang from Your Bank

One of the most important relationships you'll have during college is your relationship with your bank. Your checking account, savings account, student loans, ATM card, and credit cards all involve your bank. Here's how to keep your relationship healthy and your banking costs low.

883. Most banks offer four types of accounts: checking, savings, money market, and certificates of deposit. A checking account is a must for college students. A savings account is a good idea if you receive student loan money or financial aid money in a lump and will be using it over the course of the semester, or even if you just want to tuck away a little money for emergencies. Make your money work a little harder for you by choosing an account that will pay interest.

884. With a checking account, you can get an Automated Teller Machine (ATM) card, which gives you instant access to your cash. Choose a bank that gives you unlimited free ATM access without any fees.

885. Some banks offer a special kind of ATM card, called a debit card, which you use to make purchases instead of using cash or a check. Using debit cards saves the expense of having checks printed and can help you control your spending. They're convenient, there are no fees, they give you instant access to your money, and they limit your spending to what you actually have in your account. This is a good thing.

886. Guard your debit card carefully, and don't leave it lying around. Some debit cards require only a signature instead of a PIN number when making a purchase. If you have this kind of card and it gets into the wrong hands, someone could forge your signature and steal your money.

887. Some banks offer free checking to students, so ask around before setting up an account. Call or visit several banks, ask about their student checking accounts, and get a list of fees, interest rates, and branch locations so you can make the choice that best suits your needs.

888. When choosing a bank, ask about fees. Some banks charge a flat monthly fee for checking accounts, some charge a fee only if your account drops below a certain minimum balance, and others charge a fee for each check you write or each deposit you make. Choose the best account based on your personal situation and how you intend to use the account. For example, if you write lots of checks, you'll want an account that has a flat fee; if you write very few, it may be cheaper to pay for each check.

889. Some checking accounts pay interest, but usually require a higher minimum balance. If you're going to have low balances at certain times of the month, it might be cheaper to pay a flat fee in order to have an account with a lower minimum balance.

890. As soon as you arrive on campus, decide on a bank and set up an account so you'll have access to your money without having to pay transfer fees from home.

891. If you're unsure how to balance your checkbook each month, record ATM transactions, or write checks, ask the bank staff to show you how. A good understanding of these activities can prevent you from making costly mistakes.

892. If you use an ATM card to access your bank account, plan ahead so you can avoid incurring ATM fees at out-of-network ATMs. Why pay money to access your own funds?

893. Don't use the ATM to check your balance or review recent transactions unless you're sure your bank doesn't charge a fee for this service. Most banks provide other methods for you to check this information, either online or through an automated telephone system.

894. If you don't have enough money in your bank account to cover a check you've written, the check will bounce (be returned by the bank for insufficient funds) and your bank will charge you a fee of $25 to $35. If you wrote the check out to a business, they'll add their fee to the bank's, for a total of up to $100 or more. To prevent this, balance your checkbook, record all your ATM withdrawals and debit card transactions, record any automatic deductions, and double-check your math in your check register.

895. Sign up for overdraft protection; then resolve not to use it except to cover you when you make an error in your checkbook. You'll be protected from bouncing checks when you do make a mistake, so you'll avoid fees for insufficient funds, which usually start at $25 per check.

896. Balance your checkbook every month. Banks do make errors. More likely, though, you'll make an error in your checkbook or forget to deduct an ATM withdrawal. Balancing your checkbook can help prevent any nasty surprises and overdrawn accounts resulting in yet more fees.

897. When balancing your checkbook, be sure to add any interest you earned to your checkbook register balance and deduct any fees so your checkbook register is always up to date. Even being off a dollar can result in bounced checks.

898. You've heard the dumb blond joke: "I can't be overdrawn on my bank account. I still have checks left!" Just because you have checks doesn't mean you have money in your account, so keep your checkbook register up to date and know how much you have in your account before writing a check, using your debit card, or making a withdrawal.

899. When writing a check, fill in all of the blank spaces and draw a line through the blank unused portion. Write the check amount as a number in the box provided, and spell it out on the long line below. These precautions will help prevent your check amounts from being altered.

900. Always sign your checks as you write them. Never sign a blank check. If you make a mistake, write "VOID" in large letters across the check or shred it so nobody else will be able to use it. Note the voided check in your checkbook register and write a new one to replace the one you voided.

901. Don't use an easy-to-guess personal identification number (PIN) for your ATM, like your birthday or part of your phone number or social security number. If you lose your card, it will be very easy for someone to drain your bank account if they can easily guess your PIN.

902. Never give your bank account number or other information printed on your checks to anyone over the phone. They can use the information to fraudulently remove money from your account by submitting what's known as an electronic (paperless) check.

903. Question your bank's fees. They may seem like small potatoes, but they're big business for banks. If your bank charges a fee for a certain service, make sure it's something you really need, even if it's only a few dollars a month.

904. If your bank charges you to talk to a live teller, change banks. Originally, ATMs were supposed to save banks money by letting you do simple banking without using a live teller; then banks started charging fees to use the ATM. Now some banks are charging a fee if you use a live teller. Never pay a fee to access your own money.

905. Online banking makes it easy to keep your checkbook register up-to-date because you can quickly scan the recent activity in your account and spot any ATM withdrawals or debit card purchases you forgot to record. Don't rely solely on your online balance, though, because checks you've written may not have cleared yet, so your balance is rarely what shows up online.

906. Don't pay bank fees for check printing. Your bank will give you a small supply of starter checks. Order additional checks from a discount check printer for a fraction of the cost. Try Checks Unlimited (www.checksunlimited.com) at 1-800-204-2244, Checks in the Mail (www.checksinthemail.com) at 1-800-733-4443, or CheckWorks (www.checkworks.com) at 1-800-971-4223.

907. Avoid using nonbank ATMs whenever possible. Scammers sometimes install scanning devices in ATMs that track your PIN and account numbers. The scammers then remove all the money from your account.

908. Never write your PIN number in a conspicuous place or give the number out to anyone. It's like giving them a license to steal from you.

909. Make sure you know whether your bankcard is a debit card or a credit card. They're used interchangeably, but when you use your debit card, the money comes out of your checking account right away. If you're not aware of this, you could overdraw your account and incur a bank fee.

910. Debit cards are a great way to control your spending without carrying a lot of cash around with you, because you can only spend what you have in your checking account. This prevents the build-up of credit card debt and interest expense.

911. Just because your bank account balance shows you have enough money available to cover checks you've written or are about to write doesn't mean you won't bounce a check. Ask your bank how long they hold deposited checks before the funds are actually available to you, and then plan accordingly when writing checks or using your debit card. This will help you avoid bounced checks or overdraft fees.

912. If you bounce a check, and you've never done it before, call your bank and ask them to waive the fee. Many banks will do this for your first offense. A quick phone call is worth the potential $25 to $39 savings.

913. If you've used your credit card responsibly for at least a year, call your credit card company and ask them to lower the interest rate. Many will do so.

914. If your bank merges with or is bought by another bank, call and ask about any changes in fees and policies. You'll probably receive notices stuffed in the envelope with your bank statement, but you could easily throw these away without being aware that the bank merger could be costing you money in additional fees or higher interest rates.

915. Be sure to transfer money from your savings account to your checking account before using your debit card. If your accounts are linked, your bank may charge a fee to make this transfer for you when your checking balance is too low to cover the debit charges.

916. Keep your money in the bank, not in your pocket. It's too easy to spend impulsively when you have easy access to cash.

917. Stay away from check-cashing stores. Their fees take a bite out of your budget.

918. Take advantage of the magic of compounding. Money saved in an interest-bearing account will grow more quickly because you earn interest on both the principal and the previously earned interest. The more frequently the compounding is performed, the more money you'll end up with. Over time the difference can be significant, so don't hide your cash under your mattress or in the cookie jar.

919. Keep close tabs on the whereabouts of your ATM card and report a lost or stolen card to your bank immediately. If you report the card missing before it's used without your permission, you'll be protected against unauthorized withdrawals.

920. Before setting up a bank account in your college town, find out if there's an on campus credit union. You may get better deals on interest rates and loans, pay lower fees, and earn higher interest on deposits.

921. Bounced checks not only result in costly fees, they can show up in your credit report and may make it difficult for you to open a checking account in the future. Banks don't like customers with a history of bouncing checks.

922. By federal law, your liability for unauthorized use of your bankcard is limited to $50 if you report your card's loss within two business days, and $500 if you report the card's loss within more than two but less than 60 days. If you discover your card is missing, don't hesitate to report it.

923. "Free" checking often comes with a hidden price. The money you leave in your account to meet the minimum balance requirements for free checking could be earning interest in an interest-bearing account. If your minimum balance requirement for free checking is more than a five hundred dollars, check around for a better deal.

924. If you use a debit card, it's easy to lose track of the exact balance in your checking account unless you record the debits in your checkbook register immediately. Dipping below the minimum balance in your checking account, even for a day, can result in bank fees.

925. Don't write checks unless you have money in your checking account to fully cover them. The days of getting "float" on your money (the gap between the time you mail your payments and the time they clear your bank account) are gone, and e-checks are here to stay. Merchants send an electronic copy of your check to the bank instead of mailing it, so your checks clear much more quickly.

926. When choosing a bank, look for one that doesn't charge a fee to use any ATM or that reimburses you for fees charged by an ATM owned by another bank. This is a convenient perk because you won't have a limited number of ATMs that you can access free.

927. When choosing a bank, also compare the minimum balance requirements (if your balance falls below the minimum for even one day, you'll be charged a fee), availability and location of ATMs, hours of operation and convenient locations, availability of online banking, whether the bank pays interest on the balance in your checking account, and whether the bank is FDIC-insured.

928. If you bounce a check, be sure to record the vendor's bounced check fee and your bank's fee in your check register. Otherwise, you could get into a vicious circle of bouncing more checks and incurring additional fees.

929. Avoid using ATMs not in your bank's network. You could incur what's known as double-dipping fees, where you're charged a fee by a bank that's not in your network and a surcharge by your own bank on top of that. This can cost you as much as $4 just to withdraw a little cash from your account.

930. A little advance planning can help you avoid ATM fees. Use a debit or check card when you make purchases at stores and get cash back at the same time, instead of withdrawing cash from the ATM and incurring a fee.

931. Banks often lower fees for customers who use direct deposit, so sign up for direct deposit on any checks you receive regularly, like paychecks. Even if you already have a no-fee account, direct deposit will save you time and protect you from having your checks stolen.

15.

Save Money as a Nontraditional or Graduate Student

College: it's not just for kids. If you're a grad student, an adult attending college for the first time, or a returning student after a hiatus, you'll benefit from many of the other tips in this book, but there are special challenges and considerations that apply to you.

932. Take advantage of credit-for-experience programs that recognize the value of your life experiences and award credit toward an undergraduate degree, saving time and money. According to the College Board, 20 percent of students entering four-year colleges are eligible for credit in arts, languages, computer science, history, mathematics, natural sciences, or social sciences through Advanced Placement (AP) tests. Visit www.geteducated.com for details.

933. If you're contemplating going back to college full-time or enrolling for the first time as an adult, you can make the transition easier by paying off as much debt as possible before you enroll. Take a second job for a few months if that's what it takes to pay off debt so you can be prepared for the reduction in income. It's difficult to handle the expenses of college if you begin the college experience with a responsibility to repay previously incurred debts.

934. If your personal circumstances make attending college the traditional way unfeasible for you, don't despair. You can earn a legitimate degree by mail (correspondence courses) or online (distance learning), and save the money you would have had to spend on room and board and related expenses. Make sure the program you enroll in is accredited.

935. Just because you're an adult student returning to college doesn't mean you shouldn't apply for scholarships. While many are aimed at traditional students, there are some with no age restrictions. Essay contests tend to be open to anyone, and some scholarships specifically target adults. Surf online scholarship search engines like www.fastweb.com, and check out Peterson's Scholarships and Loans for Adult Students at the library or local bookstore.

936. Ask your college financial aid officer whether your school sponsors any scholarships for nontraditional students. They may also know of outside aid especially for nontraditionals.

937. If you're an adult returning to college or attending for the first time, search for scholarships geared specifically toward adult students. Many grants and scholarships are available from federal, state, and private organizations.

938. If you're a single parent, a woman, or a displaced homemaker or worker, you may be eligible for special financial aid. Check with the school's financial aid office.

939. If you participate in an employer tuition assistance plan, it behooves you to get the best grade possible. Most plans reimburse you for your tuition costs on a sliding scale based on your grade: 100 percent for an A, 90 percent for a B, 70 percent for a C, for example. The better your grade, the less money comes out of your own pocket.

940. If the courses you take are directly related to your job, you don't have to claim employer tuition reimbursements on your income tax return. If the courses aren't directly related to your job, you can still claim over $5,000 of reimbursements tax-free. See your tax advisor.

941. Sallie Mae, which provides federally guaranteed student loans, has a special type of loan available to adult students, who are often ineligible for regular student loans. The Career Education loan can be used for continuing education programs, including two-year programs and classes taken over the Internet.

942. If you're an adult student and you need to buy a computer for college, you can use a Career Education loan to pay for it.

943. If you've been laid off due to outsourcing or foreign competition, you may be eligible for funding for up to two years of retraining and two years of income while you learn new job skills under the Trade Adjustment Assistance program. Funds are limited, but you may be able to have part of your education costs covered if you decide to attend college for the first time or return to finish a degree you started years ago.

944. If you're over 60 and headed back to college, you may qualify for free tuition. Many states cover tuition costs for this age group. The exact age varies by state.

945. If you have a traditional or Roth IRA, you can take money from it penalty-free to cover higher education expenses. Talk to your tax advisor.

946. You can borrow up to 50 percent of your 401(k) savings at favorable interest rates (usually prime plus one or two percent) if you use the money for higher education. Always use caution when taking money from your retirement accounts. They should be a last resort.

947. If you've participated in corporate training programs in your job, you're a great candidate for converting your on-the-job training into college credit. If you received a certificate for training programs you attended, provide copies to the college. If not, ask your employer for a letter confirming your completion of these programs.

948. You may be able to obtain college credit if you have a professional license or credentials, such as a Certified Public Accountant, Certified Computer Programmer, Chartered Financial Consultant, etc. Ask your college about this before you register for classes—you may be able to skip a few courses and reduce your tuition expenses.

949. Beware of degree mills, which "award" meaningless degrees for a fee. All reputable programs require a reasonable amount of class attendance or online coursework. Before you shell out money for a degree, make sure the school is accredited; otherwise you'll just be wasting your hard-earned money on a meaningless piece of paper.

950. Financial aid is not just for traditional college students. It's also available for adult students returning to college or attending college for the first time. Types of financial aid available include grants, scholarships, low interest loans, co-operative education programs, tuition payment plans, and work-study opportunities. You won't get what you don't ask for, so be sure to apply and ask about any special options for nontraditional students.

951. Contact your State Higher Education Agency for information on financial aid, colleges and universities, grants, scholarships, and more. Your state might offer financial assistance programs for graduate or professional school. A list of Higher Education Agencies for each state and links to their websites is provided on the U.S. Department of Education's site at http://wdcrobcolp01.ed.gov/Programs/EROD/org_list.cfm?category_ID=SHE.

952. Once you've made the decision to attend college as an adult, take a hard look at your lifestyle and figure out where you can make changes to reduce your expenses as you adjust to living on a reduced income. Paying for college requires sacrifice for most students, but the rewards are worth it.

953. Housing costs are probably your largest expense. If you're having trouble coming up with the funds to pay for college, and you own your home, consider selling it and buying a smaller one or renting a small apartment while you're in school.

954. Get a roommate. If you own your home and plan to keep it, or even if you're just renting, sharing the space (and the expenses) with a roommate can make a big difference, not only in rent, but also in utilities, maintenance, and groceries.

955. If you have a relatively new car, consider selling it and buying a reliable but less expensive older model to reduce your car payments and insurance costs while you're in school. You could save hundreds of dollars a month in car payments plus several hundred dollars a year in insurance premiums.

956. When choosing a distance-learning program, look for hidden costs beyond the obvious costs of tuition. Many institutions have attractive tuition rates but excessively high fees. Be sure to get the big picture when it comes to costs.

957. For your degree to be meaningful and respected by potential employers, the institution you receive your distance degree from must be accredited by a recognized accrediting organization. Do your research to avoid throwing your money away on a degree that may not be recognized or respected. Also ask if the particular program of study you plan to take is accredited.

958. If you're thinking of returning to school after a long hiatus, or you're an adult attending college for the first time, consider starting out slowly by taking one or two classes while you continue working. This will give you time to assess whether this is really something you want to do and are committed to before you borrow a lot of money and incur debt. If, after a semester or two, you're sure you want to continue, then you can jump in with both feet.

959. Look for financial aid programs provided by organizations in your field of interest, like the American Medical Association if you're considering a medical degree, or the National Bar Association if you're considering a law degree.

960. Let Uncle Sam pick up part of the tab for your education. The U.S. Armed Forces offer financial aid opportunities, such as The U.S. Army student loan repayment enlistment incentive for new recruits who have already attended college and accumulated debt. If you qualify, the Army will repay up to $65,000 of your federally guaranteed loans in exchange for a three-year enlistment. Contact your local recruiter for details.

961. Some distance learning programs are simply moneymaking schemes. Before you spend a penny, make sure the school is accredited by one of the regional accreditation agencies listed at www.wcet.info/resources/publications/conguide/conguidm.htm. If you're considering taking distance learning classes from a private or industry provider instead of a school, make sure the program is recognized for college credit or certification by ACE/PONSI, the Program on Non-collegiate Sponsored Instruction. Otherwise you're throwing your money away on a degree that no employer will acknowledge.

962. If you have to work while attending graduate school, try to consolidate all of your classes into one day a week. You'll save time commuting to and from campus. You'll save money on gas or commuting. You'll reduce your stress level.

963. According to Nellie Mae, the student loan provider, the average graduate student will leave college with $7,831 of credit card debt. If you pay the monthly minimum payment of 2.5 percent at 18 percent interest, it would take 29 years to pay off that balance. In that time, you would pay an additional $11,362 in interest. Keep these numbers in mind when tempted to pay with your credit card.

964. Apply for a fellowship, which is a grant from a foundation or professional or cultural organization to cover your tuition and a small salary (stipend) while you're in graduate school. They're awarded competitively, so apply to multiple organizations and apply early.

965. Also ask your college if there's an office that administers fellowships. If there is, seek their assistance to increase your chances of qualifying.

966. Apply for an assistantship, and do it early, because they're very competitive. Assistantships involve teaching and research in a particular department, in exchange for a stipend and sometimes a tuition remission. Assistantships look good on your resume, too.

967. If you have to choose between a Teaching Assistantship and a Research Assistantship, keep in mind that Research Assistantships can often directly fund the research you need to perform for your degree. This makes them more desirable than an Assistantship.

968. Graduate students are often hired for English Language Services (ESL) programs to teach non-English speaking immigrants on a part-time basis. This might be a good source of income for you while you're in school.

969. Many schools allow full-time employees to take several classes a semester tuition-free. Check with the school you're interested in getting your graduate degree from. It may make sense to get a job there while working on your degree, if you can't afford to go to school full-time.

970. Before committing yourself to a graduate program, weigh the costs against what you hope to gain, professionally and personally. If your chosen profession has relatively low salaries, is it worth it to you to go into debt in order to get an advanced degree in that field?

971. If you're planning to attend graduate school, it's especially important to keep your credit card debt under control and your credit record in good shape. Alternative loans are available only to those with good credit.

972. If you want to attend graduate school in the future, be sure to pay your student loans from undergraduate school on time. If you are in default, you'll be unable to qualify for any additional federal financial aid.

973. When looking for stipends or funding for your graduate level research, visit the websites of federal agencies such as the Environmental Protection Agency (EPA), the U.S. Department of Agriculture (USDA), and the National Science Foundation (NSF) and look for information on calls for grant proposals.

974. If you've recently graduated from a four-year college and are about to enter graduate school, consider consolidating your student loans now, if rates are favorable. The extra money this generates (because of lower monthly payments) should be applied to your credit card balances to pay down this high-interest debt.

975. Graduate school is very expensive, but if you're a PhD candidate, you should receive some type of financial assistance from the school in the form of tuition waivers, a part-time job as a research assistant, or the opportunity to teach undergraduate courses. Contact the financial aid office and the head of your department.

976. When choosing a graduate school, evaluate the financial aid offers in light of the cost of living in the city or town the school is located in. A $15,000 research assistant stipend will go a lot further in a smaller town than it will in a major city like New York.

977. Contact national, regional, and local organizations for information about graduate fellowships. Check with community organizations in your town, like Rotary, Kiwanis, Altrusa, the Optimist Club, etc. Also check college honor societies, fraternities, and sororities, as well as the national offices of organizations you belong to.

978. You're likely to receive as much financial assistance for graduate school from the school itself as from federal financial aid sources. In addition to contacting the financial aid office at the school you'd like to attend, also contact the Department Chair or the Director of Graduate Studies for the department of your field of interest and ask about available financial aid.

16.

Smart Thinking at Tax Time

It's never smart to pay more taxes than you're legally required to, but to avoid doing so you need to know a little bit about the provisions of the tax laws that affect you. If you're a student or the parent of a student, there are special tax benefits you may be able to take advantage of to reduce your tax burden and put some money back in your pocket.

979. If you're unmarried and your parents (or someone else) claim you as a dependent, you have to file a tax return if you have earned income (wages, tips, taxable scholarship and fellowship grants) of more than $4,750, unearned income (interest, dividends, capital gains) of more than $750, or if your gross income is more than $750 and exceeds your earned income by more than $250. If you worked at all during the year and had taxes withheld, file a tax return even if your income was less than $4,750. You should get back everything you paid in. Depending on how much you worked, it could be a nice chunk of change, but even if it's only a few bucks, it's yours.

980. If you find income tax returns intimidating, contact your school's business department and ask about tax assistance from accounting students, or call your local IRS office for free assistance. Call early, because the closer you get to the April 15 filing deadline, the longer it will take to get help.

981. You may be able to deduct up to $2,500 in interest expense you paid on student loans used for tuition, as long as the federal government didn't subsidize the loans. Subsidized loans are those that the federal government pays the interest on while you're in school. Be sure to use form 1040 or 1040A to qualify for the interest deduction (not form 1040EZ).

982. Check with your parents to see if they plan to claim you as a dependent on their tax return. They're entitled to do so if they pay at least half of your expenses; however, if they claim you and you also claim yourself, you'll be hearing from the IRS. Save yourself the grief by communicating with your parents about this.

983. Besides the issue of whether your parents claim you on their tax return or you claim yourself, there are other tax issues to coordinate with your parents. Because they're in a higher tax bracket, they'll benefit more from the deductions and credits that may be available to you. If that's the case, taking those yourself would be shortsighted. Why save hundreds of dollars when you could save thousands?

984. If your parents claim you as a dependent on their tax return, they receive any tax credit or deduction you may be eligible for; if nobody claims you on their return, you can take the credit or deduction yourself. Make a deal with your parents to let them take the credit but slip you some of the savings in cash.

985. If you're covered as a dependent on your parents' health insurance policy, you could be risking your eligibility if you claim yourself on your income tax return. You can't be your parents' dependent for insurance purposes and be independent for tax purposes.

986. Uncle Sam has provided three education tax credits or deductions: the Hope Scholarship, the Lifetime Learning Credit, and the Higher Education Expenses Deduction. Either you or your parents can take one of them, so read up about them so you make the choice that will save you or your parents the most money.

987. If you're eligible for the Hope Scholarship Credit, you can take a credit of up to $1,500 against your income taxes (or your parents' income taxes) for the first two years of post-secondary education (college or vocational school). You'd have to pay for at least $2,000 of qualifying education expenses with money from an account other than a Coverdell, 529 savings plan, or prepaid tuition plan, and your income (or your parents' income) must be below the threshold. See the IRS website for details.

988. If you're eligible for the Lifetime Learning Credit, you can write off 20 percent of your tuition and fees (up to $2,000) for undergraduate, graduate, and professional degree courses. To claim the full Lifetime Learning Credit on your income tax return, you'd have to pay for at least $10,000 of qualifying education expenses with money from an account other than a Coverdell, 529 savings plan, or prepaid tuition plan. Your income (or your parents' income) must be below the threshold. People of all ages can qualify for this credit.

989. You or your parents can claim either the Hope Scholarship Credit or the Lifetime Learning Credit, but not both. If necessary, consult a tax expert to find out which one will benefit you or your parents most.

990. In 2004 and 2005, if your adjusted gross income is under $65,000 (for singles) and $130,000 (for married filing jointly), you can claim your actual tuition and fees up to $4,000 under the Higher Education Expenses Deduction as long as you're enrolled in an accredited public, private, or proprietary institution above the high school level. If your income is higher than these limits, but less than $80,000 (for singles) and $160,000 (for married filing jointly), you can deduct up to $2,000.

991. To claim the Higher Education Expenses Deduction, include the total you paid for tuition and other eligible costs, up to $3,000 (in 2004) on the bottom of page 1 of your form 1040 Income Tax Return. The deduction will actually depend on your tax bracket, so your parents would probably net more of a benefit than you would, if they can claim you as a dependent.

992. If you qualify for an education tax credit or deduction, make sure you choose the one that will put the most cash back in your pocket. A tax deduction reduces the income your taxes are calculated on, but a tax credit reduces your actual tax. To help you determine your eligibility for these tax deductions and credits so you can chose the one that saves you the most money, see IRS Publication 970: Tax Benefits for Higher Education.

993. If you're still your parent's dependent for tax purposes, you're probably a legal resident of your home state, not your school's state. Make sure you know your legal residency, because that's where you'll have to file your state income tax return. If you file in the wrong state, you may end up owing taxes and having to go through the hassle of correcting and refiling tax returns.

994. Keep track of where your tuition money comes from, for tax purposes. If you take a deduction or credit on your tax return for education expenses, you can't count expenses that were paid for with money from a 529 account or Coverdell education savings account, because these accounts are already tax-free. If your tuition expenses exceed the amount paid from these accounts, you can claim the excess.

995. Know what tax benefits are available to you for education expenses. Order Publication 4: Student's Guide, Publication 508: Educational Expenses 508, and Publication 520: Scholarships and Fellowships free from the IRS and educate yourself about how to take advantage of education-related tax breaks.

996. If you're legally independent from your parents (meaning you cannot be claimed as their dependent) and earn less than the income limit, you may qualify for the Earned Income Credit, a tax credit you can receive in your income tax refund or in your paycheck on a week-to-week basis. Check IRS Publication 596 to see if you're eligible.

997. Don't overpay your taxes by claiming grants and loans as income unnecessarily. If a grant paid for room and board, it's taxable and you'll have to claim it as income on your tax return, but other grants and loans are generally not taxable. Read the fine print, and consult a tax expert if necessary.

998. If you're in a work-study program that provides a break on tuition costs, or if you work in exchange for other financial aid instead of a paycheck, the benefit to you is considered income. You'll have to claim it as income and pay taxes on it when you file your tax return. If you receive a paycheck, the income will be reported on your W-2 and taxes will be withheld as you go, so you won't have to make any adjustments on your tax return.

999. Take advantage of free electronic income tax return filing services. The IRS website has a list of providers and a description of who qualifies. Most students qualify for free use of the online software and the filing fee.

1000. Don't fall for income tax refund loans, which allow you to receive an immediate short-term loan in the amount of your income tax refund, for a hefty fee. These loans typically speed up your refund by only two weeks. You can achieve the same result yourself just by filing electronically and having your refund deposited directly into your bank account.

Index

B

banking 298, 301, 304–306, 308

    checking account 209, 296

        ATM 296, 298, 299, 302, 303, 306, 308, 309

        checkbook 300, 307, 308

        checks 299, 301, 302, 304–307

        direct deposit 309

        fees 297, 309

        free checking 297, 307

        interest 298, 305

        PIN number 301, 303

theft 306

fees 301, 302

online banking 302

savings account 2, 12, 117, 192, 202, 212, 296

budget, creating 150, 157, 159

additional costs 152

chat rooms 239

emergency funds 156

entertainment 151

expenses 150

managing 158, 159

receipts 158, 190

tracking 152, 159, 161

methods 153, 154

needs 151, 160

organization 157

perspective 155, 158

saving 154, 156

software 154

unexpected expenses 155

C

charge cards 93

College Board 20, 25, 312

college fees 141, 206

applications 141

appointments 143

athletic fees 182

classes 141, 194, 207

dorm room 144, 182, 207

ID card 143, 208
late fees 142
parking 143, 185, 278, 279, 280
tuition 143
college, choosing 124
community college 125
major 125
night classes 125
tuition 124, 126
college, cutting costs 127, 128, 131
Advanced Placement 127, 312
College Level Examination Program 127
Dantes Subject Standardized Tests 127
debt, paying off 312
discount classes 132
distance learning 129, 312
Excelsior College Exams 127
summer classes 129
transferring credit 130
tuition discounts 23
tuition lock-in 134
college, paying for 126
deferred payment plans 126
tuition 132
tuition assistance plan 133
computer, buying 178, 208, 209
needed features 178
school requirements 179
student discounts 179
consignment stores 15
Coverdell Education Savings Accounts 34
credit cards 16, 60, 61, 63, 65–68, 70, 71, 142

"rule of 72" 87

Annual Percentage Rate (APR) 59

automatic payments 86

bad credit 93, 104

bankruptcy 106

common misconceptions 59, 64, 69, 76–80, 83,
 84

comparing cards 90, 91, 94, 95

controlling use 72–74, 82, 93, 95

credit report 58, 60, 81, 96, 104, 105, 107, 194,
 212

debt 60, 62, 66, 69, 72, 97

department store 83

FICO score 59

finance charge 96

identity theft 97, 98, 99, 100, 101, 193

insurance 253, 255

interest rate 64, 71, 72, 78, 81, 83, 91, 94, 304

late payments 85, 90

scams 92

transferring balance 88

D

debit cards 16, 63, 296, 303, 305, 307
 safety 297

E

EFC 20

F

FAFSA 3, 24, 26
    deadline 25
    filing 27
    renew 27
financial aid 18, 29
    additional funding 20, 29
        Air force 28
        AmeriCorps 31
        Army National Guard 31
        U.S. Army 28
        U.S. military 28
        veterans 28
    communication 18
    fine print 22
    income 34
    income change 23
    income, effect of 22
    maximizing eligibility 32, 33, 34
    out-of-pocket costs 21, 22
    process 19
    requirements 55
    special circumstances 35, 36
    time 18, 19

financial aid application 24
    deadline 27
    follow-up 26
    online submission 26
financial literacy 148, 149
    books 149
    Students in Free Enterprise (SIFE) 149
fraternities 267
    fees 267, 268
    meals 268
full-time student 127

G

graduate students 312
    adjusting 317
    assistantships, applying 322
    computer 314
    correspondence courses 312
    course credit 312, 316
    debt 323
    distance learning 312, 318–320
    financial aid 313, 317, 319, 324, 325
        employer tuition reimbursements 314
        fellowships 321, 325
        loans 314, 321, 323, 324
        scholarships 313
        senior citizens 315
        State Higher Education Agency 317
        U.S. Army 320

graduate level research 323

graduate students 315

housing costs 318

    roommates 318

returning students 319

Trade Adjustment Assistance 315

transportation 318

working 312, 320, 322

I

in-state tuition 130, 131

insurance policies 14

internet shopping 176

    paying 177

    privacy policy 176

    secure website 176

IRA 191, 315

L

loans 29, 110, 111, 133, 175, 188

    Consolidation loan 30

    managing 115–122

    Perkins loan 30, 117

    seeking help 120

    Stafford loan 29, 117

    subsidized 115

    unsubsidized 115, 120

    warnings 112–114

local scholarships 41
    chamber of commerce 42
    guidance counselor 42
    newspapers 42

M

money-saving tips 182
    apartment 182, 199, 217–219, 221, 223, 224, 229
        campus-owned 223
        commuting 224
        furnishing 225, 261
        lease 222, 223, 224, 227
        pets 222
        rent 226, 227
        renters insurance 222
        roommates 224, 225, 228
        security deposit 222, 226, 227
        utility bills 219–221, 225, 228, 237, 238, 245
    books 186
    car 185, 186, 190, 196, 206, 221, 280, 281, 285
        gasoline 281, 282, 283, 285, 286
        insurance 251, 252, 253, 284, 287, 288
        oil 283
        purchasing 285, 286
        repairs 282
        tickets 283, 284

clothing 244–250

    laundry 244–248

debts 191

dorm room 198, 216, 217, 227, 259, 261

    co-operative housing 217, 226

    Resident Assistant 216

food 228

    alcohol 258

    bulk, buying in 230, 234, 236

    comparing prices 230, 232, 234, 237

    cooking 230, 231, 233, 235

    coupons 229, 232

    eating out 183, 231, 234, 235, 236, 263

    generic brands 233, 234

    grocery shopping 229–232, 235

    meal plans 228, 232

freebies 198, 200, 262, 266, 293

income tax refund 188, 190

insurance 253, 254, 255

internet 210

living at home 218, 226

mail 196, 203

non-essentials 259, 260

    CDs 258

    coffee 259

    concerts 260

    dates 264

    gambling 259, 260

    games 263

    gift cards 192, 194

    greeting cards 186

    hair 182, 184, 202

magazines 266

movies 260, 262–265

music 264, 266, 267, 294

photos 187

smoking 212, 259

tanning 183

TV 265

school supplies 187, 206

sex 189

telephone bill 238, 240, 242, 244

cell phone 238, 240–243

instant messaging 239

internet phone services 239

landline phone 239

long-distance 238, 242, 243

phone card 241

borrowing 203

N

national scholarships 45

athletic scholarships 49

Coca-Cola Scholars 46

community college transfer 47

Elks National Foundation 46

Gates Foundation 45

Intel Science Talent Search 48

Siemens Westinghouse Competition 47

Zonta International 45

non-traditional students 312

401(k) 315

college credit 316
  Advanced Placement tests 312
correspondence courses 312
distance learning 312, 319, 320
employer tuition assistance 314
financial aid 317, 319
  loans 314, 321
    Sallie Mae 314
  scholarships 313
  senior citizen 315
  special financial aid 313
  State Higher Education Agency 317
  U.S. Armed forces 320
housing costs 318
  roommates 318
IRA 315
returning students 319
tax return 314
Trade Adjustment Assistance 315
transportation 318
work 320

O

odd jobs 5–12
off-campus jobs 4, 128
offbeat scholarships 43
  "Stuck at the Prom" contest 44
  duck calling contest 43
  heritage scholarship 43
  Tall Clubs 43

on-campus jobs 3, 134
out-of-state tuition 130

P

part-time jobs 3
part-time students 21, 195
payday loans 195
PROFILE form 25

S

savings bonds 13
scholarship tips 49
    career-related 52
    deadlines 50
    essays 50
    grades 51
    local 53
    scams 51, 52
    siblings 53
    timing 49
scholarships 29
    adult students 313
    books 39
    college awards 38
    ethnic groups 41
    income 54
    internet 40
        databases 40

FastWeb 40

labor union 39

parents' employers 38

Peace Corps 30

private foundations 41

requirements 55

ROTC 30, 132

sports 54

seeking help 102–104

smart card 63

sororities 267

fees 267, 268

meals 268

spending habits 146

awareness 146

compulsive spending 147, 164, 197, 198

enhancing mood 147, 258

psychological counseling 147

spending, controlling 162, 201

advertising 164, 166, 172

avoiding sales 162, 175, 212

bulk buying 172, 173

comparing 163, 166, 168, 169

discount stores 170, 182, 200, 208, 261

haggling 167

off-brands 164, 165, 169, 171, 173, 183, 184

online shopping 185

patience 166, 174, 199, 201, 211, 213

research 162

restaurants 183, 192, 200, 201

salespeople 165, 167, 203

scams 167, 168, 169, 175

urges 165

stocks 14

student discounts 290, 292

    college newspaper 291

    college towns 291, 292, 293

    coupon books 291

    software 293

    Student Advantage card 290

    student ID 290, 293

    websites 290, 291, 292

student loans 23

summer job 2

    overtime 2

T

taxes 328

    benefits 333

    claims 329

        dependent 330, 333

        independent 334

    deductions 329, 330

        education expenses 333

        Higher Education Expenses Deduction
            332

        Hope Scholarship Credit 331

        Lifetime Learning Credit 331

    filing return 328

        assistance 328

        electronic filing 335

      grants 334

      loans 334, 335

      W-2 form 334

      work-study 334

textbooks 134

      borrow 139

      buy 135, 136, 138, 139, 140

      online 137, 138, 140

      rent 139

      sell 134, 137, 140, 141

travel 269

      airlines 270–276

      baggage 277

      bus 273, 274

      foreign country 271

      hidden fees 270

      holidays 270

      planning 271, 272, 275

      scams 277

      spring break 269, 270

      summer break 270

      train 272, 274

U

unclaimed money 13

W

work-study 2, 3, 334

About the Author

Debby Fowles is an accountant, author, freelance writer, and small business consultant. As the About.com Guide for Financial Planning since 1998, Debby has written over 150 articles about personal finance. Several of her articles have been published by Fidelity Investments and other online and print publications.

Debby served for fourteen years as controller and ten years on the board of directors of a rapidly growing biomedical research company near Washington, D.C. She has been listed in several compilations of *Who's Who*, including *Who's Who of Women Executives* (National Reference Press), *Who's Who* (Sterling), *Who's Who of Notable American Women*, and *Who's Who Registry of Business Leaders*.